I am a
# JEW

# I am a

## JEW

**Clive Lawton**
meets
**Ilana Goldman**

**Photography: Chris Fairclough**

# FRANKLIN WATTS
### NEW YORK • LONDON • SYDNEY

Ilana Goldman is ten years old. She and her family are Jews. They live in Kenton, which is just outside London. Her father, Herschel, is a civil servant. Her mother, Evelyn, sells Jewish books from a little shop that she runs in their home. Ilana has one brother, Adam, who is twelve.

# Contents

© 1984 Franklin Watts
Paperback edition 1993
This edition 1997

Franklin Watts
96 Leonard Street
London EC2A 4RH

Franklin Watts Australia
14 Mars Road
Lane Cove
NSW 2066

The Publishers would like to
thank the Goldman family and
all other people shown in this book.

Text Editor:Brenda Clarke
Design: Peter Benoist
Illustration: Tony Payne

ISBN: 0 86313 139 5 (hardback)
ISBN: 0 7496 1403 X (paperback)

Printed in Hong Kong

## Being Jewish

**I was born a Jew so I cannot remember when I first thought about it. But there are many special occasions in the year that remind me of my religion.**

Although there are some converts to the Jewish religion most Jews are born into the Jewish people. It is like a very big family. Each year there are many customs and traditions that teach Jews about their history and beliefs.

**We have many chances to give presents which remind us to look after other people.**

The Jewish religion is a family and community religion so the home and the Jewish community centre, the synagogue, are both very important. All the time, Jews try to remember God and make even ordinary things, like food, special. To show respect to God Jewish men cover their heads, particularly when saying prayers. The little hat that many of them wear is called a kipa.

## Shabbat – the special day

**Every week our special day, Shabbat, starts on Friday evening when mother lights the candles.**

Shabbat starts at sunset every Friday. It is a day of joy and rest. To show that this is a bright and festive day, candles are always lit by the mother. She thanks God when she lights them and covers her eyes as she says a prayer.

**After mother has lit the candles, father gives us a blessing from the Bible.**

The same blessing was given in the Temple at Jerusalem 2000 years ago. It asks God to look after everybody and bless them with peace. The Jewish Bible is the same as the Old Testament used by Christians.

We use our best things for the three Shabbat meals. Supper starts with a cup of wine to celebrate our special day. Between courses we sing Shabbat songs.

Drinking a cup of wine is a Jewish way of celebrating. There is a special blessing to thank God for the wine. Shabbat table songs and prayers give thanks for the food.

**On Saturday evening, when Shabbat ends, I hold the special candle at Havdalla. Adam always holds the spice box.**

Havdalla marks the end of Shabbat. The cup of wine is filled to overflowing, to show that the joy of Shabbat should "spill over" to the new week. The scent of spices is breathed in to try and continue the feeling of Shabbat.

## Jewish food laws

**One way we remember God is by being careful about our food. For example, when I buy sweets, I make sure that the ingredients are kosher.**

The Bible has many rules about food. When food fits all the rules it is called kosher. Some food has a sign on the packet which guarantees that it is kosher. Otherwise, many Jews will check the ingredients on the packet very carefully.

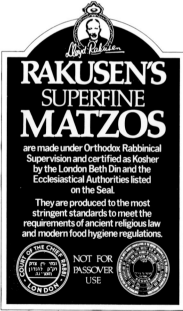

**RAKUSEN'S SUPERFINE MATZOS**

are made under Orthodox Rabbinical Supervision and certified as Kosher by the London Beth Din and the Ecclesiastical Authorities listed on the Seal.

They are produced to the most stringent standards to meet the requirements of ancient religious law and modern food hygiene regulations.

NOT FOR PASSOVER USE

**Every festival has something special to eat. For Shabbat we either make our own plaited bread or we buy it from a kosher bakery.**

One rule is that food with meat in it must be kept apart from food with milk or dairy products in it. Kosher kitchens have two separate sets of plates, pots and cutlery – one for milk and one for meat foods. Ilana's kitchen even has two sinks. Because of special rules about meat, Jews buy their meat from a kosher butcher. Food which contains animal fats or meat must also be guaranteed kosher.

## The synagogue and rabbi

Every Saturday morning we go to our synagogue. My favourite part of the service is when the big scroll is taken out of the Ark and paraded round. My father goes to synagogue every day.

Each synagogue has a rabbi who teaches Jews to live according to Jewish traditions. He also leads the people in looking after the poor, the old and the sick. Any man in the synagogue can lead services.

14

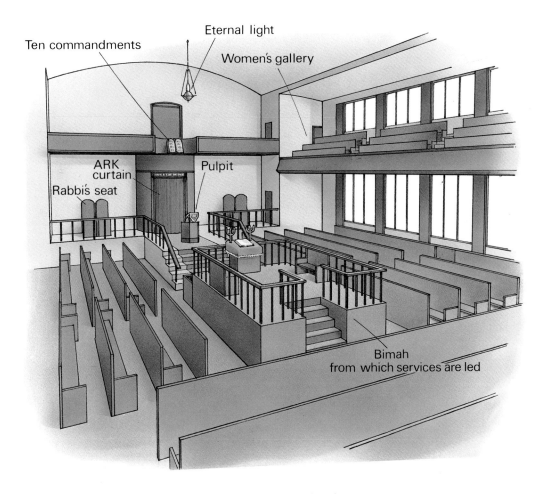

Ten commandments

Eternal light

Women's gallery

ARK curtain

Pulpit

Rabbi's seat

Bimah
from which services are led

**Men and women sit separately in my synagogue. The prayers are led from a platform in the middle. This is called the Bimah.**

The picture shows the part of the synagogue in which services are held. A synagogue is also the place where Jewish people gather for meetings and parties. So the building has a hall with a kitchen and classroom.

## Learning Jewish customs

On Sunday mornings I go to our synagogue religion school. I also go on Tuesday and Wednesday evenings after school. We learn Hebrew, Jewish history and Bible stories. We make things for the festivals and sing Hebrew songs.

It is important for Jews to know about their traditions. There is a lot to learn – the Hebrew language, 3500 years of history, customs for more than a dozen festivals, the food laws, and all the teachings and stories in the Bible.

## Hebrew

The Hebrew alphabet has only 22 letters and no vowels. Five letters are written differently if they come at the end of a word (inside box). Hebrew is written from right to left so if this were a Hebrew book it would start at the other end. Hebrew is the language in which the Bible was first written. It is also the language of Israel today.

V H D G B Silent

אבגדהו

L KH Y T KH Z

זחטיכל

P/F Silent S N M

מנסעפ

T S/SH R K TZ

צקרשת

TZ P/F N M KH

ךםןףץ

Shalom שלום

**Next year my brother is having his Barmitzvah. He has lessons every week to learn how to sing from the scroll of Torah. It takes a scribe about a year to write a scroll.**

When a Jewish girl is twelve she has a Batmitzvah. A boy has his Barmitzvah when he is thirteen. Now they are expected to be responsible for their actions and to follow the rules and customs of Jewish life. No longer can they claim they are "only children".

# Herschel and Evelyn's family history

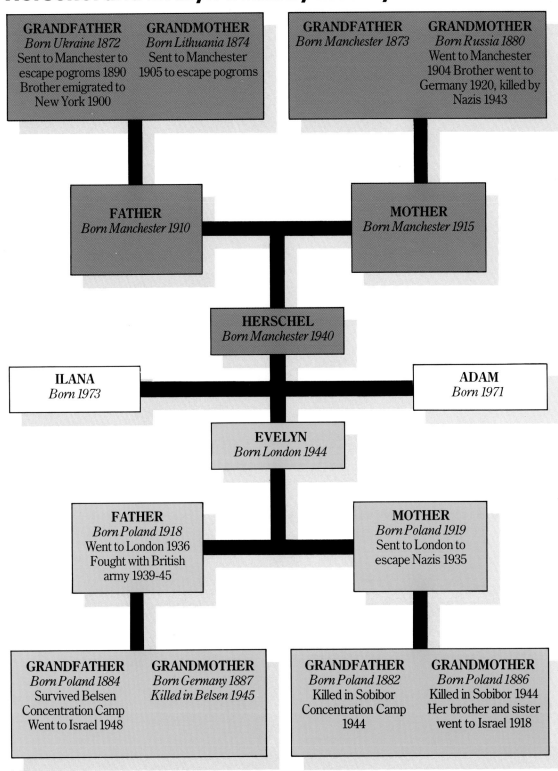

**GRANDFATHER**
*Born Ukraine 1872*
Sent to Manchester to escape pogroms 1890 Brother emigrated to New York 1900

**GRANDMOTHER**
*Born Lithuania 1874*
Sent to Manchester 1905 to escape pogroms

**GRANDFATHER**
*Born Manchester 1873*

**GRANDMOTHER**
*Born Russia 1880*
Went to Manchester 1904 Brother went to Germany 1920, killed by Nazis 1943

**FATHER**
*Born Manchester 1910*

**MOTHER**
*Born Manchester 1915*

**HERSCHEL**
*Born Manchester 1940*

**ILANA**
*Born 1973*

**ADAM**
*Born 1971*

**EVELYN**
*Born London 1944*

**FATHER**
*Born Poland 1918*
Went to London 1936 Fought with British army 1939-45

**MOTHER**
*Born Poland 1919*
Sent to London to escape Nazis 1935

**GRANDFATHER**
*Born Poland 1884*
Survived Belsen Concentration Camp Went to Israel 1948

**GRANDMOTHER**
*Born Germany 1887*
*Killed in Belsen 1945*

**GRANDFATHER**
*Born Poland 1882*
Killed in Sobibor Concentration Camp 1944

**GRANDMOTHER**
*Born Poland 1886*
*Killed in Sobibor 1944*
Her brother and sister went to Israel 1918

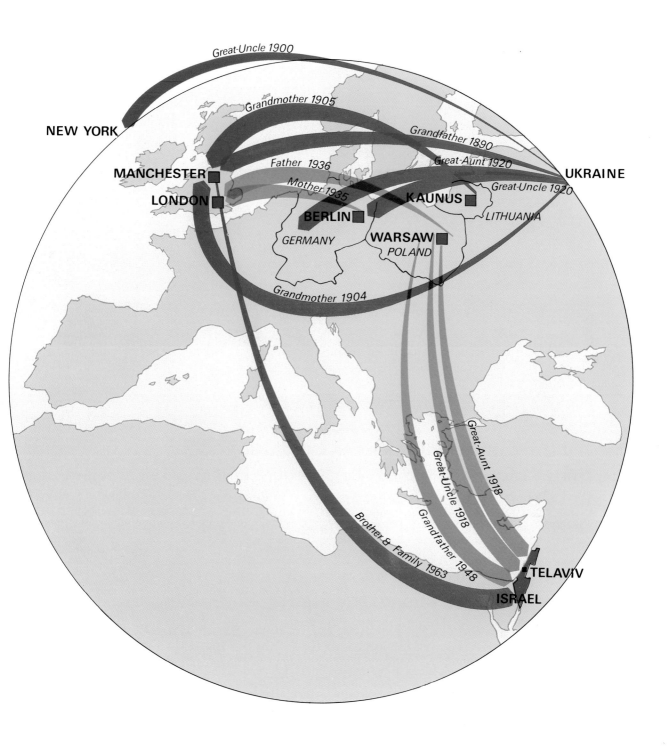

NEW YORK

Great-Uncle 1900

Grandmother 1905

MANCHESTER

LONDON

Father 1936

Mother 1935

BERLIN

Grandfather 1890

Great-Aunt 1920

UKRAINE

Great-Uncle 1920

KAUNUS

LITHUANIA

WARSAW

POLAND

GERMANY

Grandmother 1904

Great-Aunt 1918

Great-Uncle 1918

Grandfather 1948

Brother & Family 1963

TELAVIV

ISRAEL

19

## Passover – the festival of freedom

**All the family comes to us for the Seder meal at Passover. Because I am the youngest, I ask the four questions that begin the service.**

Passover comes at spring-time. The house is cleaned and all the family gathers for Seder at supper-time on the first evening of Passover. It reminds Jews of the Exodus from slavery in Egypt 3500 years ago. There is a service with questions, stories, games and songs.

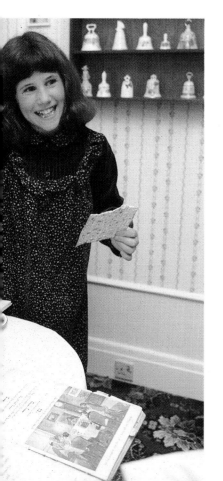

**For Seder, we have all sorts of foods that go on a special plate in the middle of the table. After supper, we must find the piece of matza hidden by my father before the service can go on.**

Among the foods eaten at Seder are bitter herbs, to remind Jews of their misery as slaves in Egypt all those thousands of years ago. There is also a flat bread called matza. This reminds Jews that in their hurry to escape, they had no time to leave the bread to rise.

21

# Sukkot – the harvest festival

**We make our Sukka by taking the roof off our garden shed. We cover the shed in leaves and branches and decorate it with fruit and pictures.**

The week-long festival of Sukkot comes in the autumn. The Sukka is a shelter. It reminds Jews that their ancestors lived in tents as they wandered in the desert on their escape from Egypt to Israel.

**During the week of Sukkot we eat all our meals in the Sukka, unless it is raining. Without the shed roof, the Sukka is open to the sky!**

Every synagogue builds a Sukka for the whole community every year. Families who have enough space in their back garden often build their own Sukka there. In Israel, many flats are specially planned so that a Sukka can be put up on the balcony. Fruit is hung in the Sukka because Sukkot is a harvest festival.

## Some other festivals

**On Simhat Torah, we take out all the scrolls from the Ark and dance around with them. The children carry flags or toy scrolls.**

Simhat Torah comes straight after Sukkot. It means "the celebrating of the Torah". Everybody goes to the synagogue. They dance and sing to celebrate having the special way of life taught in the Torah. Sometimes streamers and sweets are thrown to the children as they dance.

On Hanukka, I light my own candles. The festival lasts eight days, and on each night I light an extra candle. We play the dredle game with a spinning top and give presents to friends and family.

Hanukka is a winter festival. It celebrates the Jews winning back their Temple at Jerusalem about 2100 years ago. The story tells that the oil used for the Temple lamp had nearly all been destroyed. The little oil left lasted eight days, giving the Jews time to make more. The dredle carries Hebrew letters saying "A great miracle happened there".

# Purim – carnival time

**On Purim, the story of Esther in the Bible is read out. We all have rattles. When the name of "Haman" is said we make such a noise that it cannot be heard.**

Purim comes at the end of winter. It celebrates the time when Queen Esther saved the Jews of Persia from being killed by Haman. At this happy festival the synagogue has a carnival feeling.

**We have fancy dress parties, act plays and take plates of sweets, fruit and biscuits to friends and family.**

Purim is a time for all sorts of funny shows and plays. Some people even go to the synagogue in fancy dress. This is another festival for giving presents, especially to people who are too old or too ill to leave their homes. Jews are commanded to see that everybody can join in their happy celebrations.

27

# The Jewish Year

The Jewish calendar is lunar, which means that the months start with each new moon. Each month is only 29 or 30 days long so the whole year has only about 355 days. Seven times every 19 years a whole extra month is added, so a leap year has 13 months.

**DECEMBER**
**KISLEV**
**NOVEMBER**
**HESHVAN**
**OCTOBER**
**TISHRI**
**SEPTEMBER**
**ELUL**
**AUGUST**
**AV**
**TAMUZ**
**JULY**

### HANUKKA
(FESTIVAL OF LIGHTS)
*Kislev – 8 days*
Celebrates the winning back of the Temple of Jerusalem over 2,000 years ago and reminds one of the story of the lamp oil which miraculously lasted longer than expected.

### SUKKOT
(AUTUMN FESTIVAL)
*Tishri – 7/8 days*
Celebrates the harvest and remembers the wandering of the Jews in the desert from Egypt to Israel 3,500 years ago.

### ROSH HASHANA
(NEW YEAR)
*Tishri – 2 days*
Commemorates the birthday of the world and starts ten days of repentance for sins.

### SIMHAT TORAH
(CELEBRATING THE TORAH)
*Tishri – 1 day*
The day following Sukkot which marks the end of each year's reading of the whole Torah and the start of a new reading all over again.

### YOM KIPPUR
(DAY OF ATONEMENT)
*Tishri – 1 day*
A twenty-five hour fast which ends the ten days of repentance and gives an opportunity to make new year resolutions.

### TISHA B'AV (FAST OF AV)
*Av – 1 day*
A twenty-five hour fast during which nothing is eaten or drunk to mourn the destruction of the Temple in Jerusalem.

Calendar months around the circle:

JANUARY · TEVET · SHEVAT · FEBRUARY · ADAR · MARCH · NISAN · APRIL · IYAR · MAY · SIVAN · JUNE

## TU B'SHEVAT
(NEW YEAR FOR TREES)
*Shevat – 1 day*
Trees are planted and everybody tries to eat fifteen different kinds of fruit from trees on that day.

## PURIM
(THE CARNIVAL FESTIVAL)
*Adar – 1 day*
Celebrates the foiling of the wicked Haman's plan to destroy the Jews in Persia 2,500 years ago, as told in the book of Esther in the Bible.

## PESACH (PASSOVER)
*Nisan – 7/8 days*
Celebrates the escape from slavery in Egypt 3,500 years ago and the start of the journey to the Promised Land.

## YOM HA'ATZMAUT
*Iyar – 1 day*
Independence Day. Celebrates the founding of the State of Israel in 1948.

## SHAVUOT (PENTECOST)
*Sivan – 1/2 days*
Comes exactly seven weeks after Passover and celebrates the giving of the Torah at Mount Sinai.

# Jewish Facts and Figures

Only about 355,000 Jews live in Britain. Of these, two-thirds live in London and the rest in about 80 other towns and cities.

There are 14 million Jews in the whole world (not much more than the population of Tokyo, Japan).

About a quarter of the Jews in the world live in Israel.

Over a third of the Jews in the world live in the United States of America. Nearly 2 million live in New York.

Jews are found in about 120 countries of the world. There are Chinese, Indians and black African Jews.

Israel is about the same size as Wales.

The Jews are an ancient people with a history stretching back over 3500 years. Most Jews are born into a Jewish family, but some are converted to the Jewish religion.

Jews do not try to convert people to Judaism. They prefer others to follow their own religious traditions properly.

Israel is the country of the Jewish People. The modern state was founded in 1948.

The history of the Jewish people began in Israel. Jews still face towards its capital city – Jerusalem – when praying.

The first Jew was Abraham, whose story is told in the Bible. Other famous Jews in the Bible are Joseph, Moses, King David, King Solomon, Elijah, Isaiah and Samson.

Jews believe in one God. They try to live according to the teachings laid down in the Jewish Bible.

The Old Testament of the Christian holy book – the Bible – is the same as the Jewish holy book. So this is often called the Jewish Bible. It was originally written in Hebrew so it is sometimes called the Hebrew Bible.

The first five books of the Jewish Bible are called the Torah. This gives the basis of Jewish teaching and tells the story of the beginning of the world and the Jewish people.

The Jewish day begins and ends at sunset.

Jewish law forbids the eating of certain foods including pork and shellfish.

# Glossary

**Ark** The place in the synagogue where the scrolls of the Torah are kept.

**Batmitzvah, Barmitzvah** Words used to describe a girl or boy coming of age at 12 or 13.

**Concentration camp** A most cruel form of prison. People are crowded together with little care for whether they live or die. 6,000,000 Jews were killed in the camps set up by the Nazis in the Second World War.

**Dredle** A little spinning top.

**Kibbutz** A sort of village in Israel. People on a kibbutz often live by farming. Everybody shares what they have, including the money they earn.

**Kosher** Anything that fits Jewish law. It is mostly used about food, but can describe anything else. A Sukka without an open roof is not a kosher Sukka.

**Matza** A flat cracker made of flour and water, but no yeast. This "unleavened" bread does not rise.

**Pogrom** Riots which took place in Eastern Europe against Jewish communities.

**Rabbi** A Jewish teacher. Rabbis study for many years. They can have any sort of job, not just that of a teacher or community leader.

**Seder** The meal and service on the first evening of Passover. It recalls and acts out the story of the Jews' escape from slavery in Egypt 3500 years ago.

**Shabbat** The Jewish day of rest and celebration. It starts on Friday at sunset and ends on Saturday evening. The Christian holy day, Sunday, is also named after it.

**Sukka** A hut put up for a short time. The hut has a leafy roof built for the festival of Sukkot in the autumn.

**Synagogue** The Jewish community centre. Here daily services are held, children are taught and other events take place.

**The Temple** The Temple in Jerusalem was the central place of worship for Jews. It was built by King Solomon about 2700 years ago and destroyed by the Romans 800 years later. The building has gone, but part of the Western Wall still stands.

# Index

32 Fife COUNCIL

King's Road Primary School
Rosyth - Tel: 313470

USBORNE CASTLE TALES

# THE ROYAL BROOMSTICK

## Heather Amery
## Illustrated by Stephen Cartwright

Language consultant: Betty Root
Series editor: Jenny Tyler

There is a little yellow duck to find on every page.

# This is Grey Stone Castle.

This is King Leo and Queen Rose. They have two children called Prince Max and Princess Alice.

Today it is raining.

"What shall we do?" says Max. "Let's go up to see Queen Gran in her tower," says Alice.

Max and Alice climb the stairs to the tower.

The room is empty. "Where's Queen Gran?"
asks Alice. "She must have gone out," says Max.

"There's a broomstick."

"Let's pretend it's a horse," says Alice. "Queen Gran says we mustn't touch anything," says Max.

# Alice gets on the broomstick.

"Look, Max, it's moving. Quick, get on," says Alice. The broomstick flies around the room.

"What shall we do?"

"Hold on tight," says Max. They fly out of the window and around the top of the tower.

"Where are we going?"

"How do you steer a broomstick?" asks Max.
"I don't know but I'm not scared," says Alice.

The broomstick flies on.

It flies near a very tall tree. "Look!" says Max.
"I can see something moving in the tree."

"It's Lucky, Queen Gran's cat."

"Poor Lucky is stuck and she can't get down,"
says Alice. The broomstick stops near the cat.

The cat jumps on.

"Hold on, Lucky," says Alice. "You're safe now."
"Take us home please, broomstick," says Max.

They all fly back to the castle.

The broomstick whizzes through the window
and stops. Max, Alice and Lucky jump off.

"That was fun," says Max.

"Quick, put the broomstick back in the corner,"
says Alice. "I can hear someone coming."

Queen Gran comes in.

"There you are, my dears," she says. "I hope you have been good and not touched anything."

"Oh! There's Lucky."

"I have been looking for her everywhere,"
says Queen Gran. "I thought she was lost."

# "We've been a little naughty."

"But we did find Lucky," says Max. "It was
the broomstick which found her," says Alice.

First published in 1996 by Usborne Publishing Ltd, 83-85 Saffron Hill, London EC1N 8RT, England. Copyright © Usborne Publishing Ltd.
The name Usborne and the device ⚭ are Trade Marks of Usborne Publishing Ltd. All rights reserved. No part of this publication may be reproduced,
stored in a retrieval system, or transmitted in any form or by any means, electronic, mechanical, photocopy, recording or otherwise, without prior
permission of the publisher. UE First published in America in August 1996. Printed in Italy.

# Pottery

# Pottery

JOHN GALE

teach yourself®

*Dedication*
*To Barbara, Nicholas and Emma*

For UK order enquiries: please contact Bookpoint Ltd, 130 Milton Park, Abingdon, Oxon OX14 4SB. Telephone: (44) 01235 827720, Fax: (44) 01235 400454. Lines are open from 9.00-18.00, Monday to Saturday, with a 24-hour message answering service. You can also order through our website www.madaboutbooks.com

For USA order enquiries: please contact McGraw-Hill Customer Services, P.O. Box 545, Blacklick, OH 43004-0545, USA Telephone: 1-800-722-4726. Fax: 1-614-755-5645.

For Canada order enquiries: please contact McGraw-Hill Ryerson Ltd, 300 Water St, Whitby, Ontario L1N 9B6, Canada. Telephone: 905 430 5000. Fax: 905 430 5020.

Long renowned as the authoritative source for self-guided learning – with more than 30 million copies sold worldwide – the *Teach Yourself* series includes over 300 titles in the fields of languages, crafts, hobbies, business and education.

*British Library Cataloguing in Publication Data*
A catalogue record for this title is available from The British Library.

*Library of Congress Catalog Card Number:* On file

First published in UK 2001 by Hodder Headline Ltd, 338 Euston Road, London NW1 3BH.

First published in US 2001 by Contemporary Books, a Division of The McGraw-Hill Companies, 1 Prudential Plaza, 130 East Randolph Street, Chicago IL60601, USA.

The 'Teach Yourself' name is a registered trade mark of Hodder & Stoughton Ltd.

Cover photo from Steve Tanner
Typeset by Dorchester Typesetting Group Ltd.
Printed in Dubai for Hodder & Stoughton Educational, a division of Hodder Headline Plc, 338 Euston Road, London NW1 3BH.

Impression number    10 9 8 7 6 5 4 3 2 1
Year                          2009 2008 2007 2006 2005 2004 2003

# Contents

■ Thrown porcelain shape.

# Introduction

The purpose of this book is to help anyone who is interested in making pottery.

Pottery-making, in its widest sense, requires many skills, much technical knowledge and a lot of equipment. However, as with all creative activities, a simple technique, carried out with care, can produce a presentable result quite quickly. For example, a piece of clay from a local source could be shaped using the pinch method, burnished, and fired in a sawdust kiln in the back garden. In this way one would become involved with the basic requirements of making a pot, these being (*a*) clay; (*b*) a manipulative skill; (*c*) firing. From this simple beginning one could progress to other methods of forming and finishing.

However it soon becomes necessary to have more materials and equipment. Then comes the question of what to buy, in what quantities and where from. At the back of the book I have included lists of materials and equipment and suppliers, which should solve all these problems. However, before buying either equipment or materials, some first-hand knowledge of them is always useful. I therefore recommend a beginners' pottery course at one of the many colleges of further education. These courses are very cheap and provide the opportunity of using a variety of materials and equipment before deciding what to buy.

I have set out the text to follow the general sequence of pottery-making, beginning with clay (its origins, preparation, etc.), and concluding with firing (procedure, types of kilns, etc.). While it is necessary, therefore, to read the whole book through in order to understand the broader aspects of pottery-making, it is not necessary, at first, to understand everything in the book in order to make a good pot. Important points to know are:

- What materials, etc. to buy, where from, and in what quantities.
- How to prepare clay (kneading, wedging).
- How to work clay (pinching, slabbing, coiling, throwing).
- Methods of decorating clay (incising, sgraffito, etc.).
- How to pack a kiln for biscuit and glaze firing.
- How to fire a kiln and the use of cones.
- How to mix a glaze.
- How to colour a glaze.
- How to apply a glaze.

Finally, I offer the following advice to the beginner or indeed any potter.

- Do not expect to learn everything about pottery-making in five minutes. This is impossible and if it were not, one would lose much of the excitement of always being able to experience something new.
- Do not be in too great a hurry to achieve results.
- Always prepare materials (clays, etc.) thoroughly before using them.
- Always work in a tidy manner.
- Do not be daunted if things go wrong from time to time. Become even more determined to overcome the problems.
- Learn pottery-making step by step, do it well and above all enjoy doing it.

Now read on.

# 1

# The meaning of pottery

The word pottery is a collective term that may be used to describe anything made out of clay which has been 'fired' (heated) through a temperature of 450°C–700°C, thus losing its chemically combined water and being chemically changed into a rock-like material unable to be returned to its original clay state. An alternative word to pottery is ceramic which is of Greek origin and stems from the word 'Keramos' which means both pottery and the raw plastic clay material used in its manufacture.

## Types of pottery

I have heard many people use 'pottery' as a singular term when describing the familiar shiny glazed earthenware. Earthenware, however, is only one type of pottery and the actual glaze plays no part in the definition.

There are three different types of pottery depending on the sort of clay used in its manufacture and the amount of heat to which the dried clay has been subjected. They are earthenware, stoneware and porcelain.

### Earthenware

This is any pottery which is 'soft' (can be scratched with a metal point), opaque and porous, even if the pot has been rendered impermeable by covering the surface with a vitreous coating known as glaze. A glaze is, in fact, necessary to prevent the pot from leaking.

This category includes all primitive pottery, all terracottas (unglazed, low-fired ware), most Near-Eastern and Mediterranean pottery, some Chinese, the Japanese 'Raku' ware originating in the sixteenth century, most European pottery up to the seventeenth century and the fine white earthenware from which much of our modern tableware is made.

### Stoneware

This is any pottery which is hard (cannot be scratched with a metal point), opaque, vitreous and impermeable. It is because of its dense, hard impervious character that it is so named. Unlike earthenware, it requires a glaze only for hygienic and aesthetic reasons rather than to prevent the pot from leaking.

This category includes the Chinese porcellanous stoneware of the Han Dynasty in the first century BC (sometimes referred to as 'protoporcelain'), the salt-glazed stoneware of Europe originating in the Rhineland of Germany in the fifteenth century, the utilitarian stoneware produced in quantity in England at the beginning of the twentieth century (hot-water and ink bottles and marmalade jars, etc.), and the electrical equipment, laboratory ware and ovenware of today.

the first translucent pottery came from China.

Of these three types of pottery the one most favoured by artist potters today is undoubtedly stoneware, perhaps due to its finished quality having a natural rather than manufactured appearance, and also may be due to its vitreosity and strength. Nevertheless, all three offer the potter considerable scope for research and development. In the following text materials, methods and techniques required to produce each one will be dealt with.

## Porcelain

This is any pottery which is hard, vitreous, impermeable and translucent. The latter characteristic makes it distinguishable from stoneware.

This category includes the first porcelain of the T'ang Dynasty (AD 618–906), European porcelain originating in Meissen, Germany, at the beginning of the eighteenth century, and present-day bone china which was evolved in Staffordshire, England, by Josiah Spode towards the end of the eighteenth century. Bone china is so called because of the calcined bone (usually of oxen) used in its composition to give it translucency and strength, and also because of the fact that

■ Thrown garden stoneware.

# 2

# Clay

The two prime requirements for pottery-making are clay, in which to fashion the ware, and a kiln, in which to heat or fire it. It is interesting and indeed necessary to know something of the material with which one is working, not only to save time and frustration in fruitless experimentation but also to realize the potential of the material and to feel the excitement and satisfaction of constructive research and probable success.

■ Thrown stoneware mugs.

## Types of Clay

As the felspathic rocks from which clay is naturally produced make up three-quarters of the earth's crust, it is hardly surprising that clay is a commodity which can be found in large quantities the world over. The fact that primitive man used clay, and burnt clay ware found in excavations in the Nile Valley is said to be 13,000 years old, indicate that clay is neither difficult to find nor to fire. It is, however, quite varied in its colour, texture, plasticity, shrinkage and strength. Therefore, in order to describe the formation and varied properties of clay more fully, it is necessary to divide it into two main groups: primary clays and secondary clays.

### Primary clay

In simple terms, all clay is formed by the natural decomposition of felspar. This is a mineral generally in the form of opaque white rectangular crystals found alone as pure felspar or more commonly combined with quartz and mica as granite and gneiss. When these rocks disintegrate due to weathering and come under the influence of water and carbonic acid in conditions where there is an absence of atmospheric oxygen, the felspar is decomposed and the following process takes place: the potash and some of the silica is dissolved by water and washed away while the remaining alumina and silica combine with water to form clay (hydrated silicate of aluminium).

This clay, which is white in colour, is primary clay or first clay, and is found on or around the site of the 'mother rock' from which it was formed. As it was used in the making of vitrified white ware in China at least 1,200 years before deposits of it were discovered in Europe, it is known to us as china clay or kaolin. The latter is derived from the Chinese word 'Kao-ling', meaning 'high-ridge' which is presumably an area in China where this white clay was first found.

English china clay is mined around St Austell in Cornwall, where one can see the decomposition process in various stages with partically decomposed granite, china clay, quartz and mica all together. The china clay is obtained by playing powerful jets of water over the excavated rock face. The china clay is thus washed down to the bottom of the pit from where it is pumped into settling tanks which sort out the fine particles of clay from the coarser material.

The white pyramids dotting the countryside around St Austell are not, however, as is often thought, china-clay tips, but deposits of the waste materials. China clay, while not usually worked by itself, is indispensable in the making of pure white porcelain and is included in fine earthenware bodies. China clay or kaolin can be found in America around Alabama, Georgia and South Carolina; in Europe from the Ukraine to the Pyrenees; at Meissen in Germany; Zettlitz in Czechoslovakia; in Limoges, France, and of course in China. It is, however, relatively scarce and varies in colour and plasticity. We are therefore fortunate in England to have a deposit of unusual purity which gives outstanding whiteness in the finished ware, and being also used in papermaking, medicines, etc., it has become a valuable export.

## Secondary clays

These are primary clays which have been carried by running water, glaciers, etc., from the site of the 'mother rock' and deposited elsewhere. These clays are found in far greater quantities than primary clays and are varied in colour and texture due to impurities, such as iron, which have been picked up in transit. Secondary clays are much more 'plastic' than the primary clays due, it seems, to their finer particle size, produced by the constant milling they received while being transported from one site to another. Here, we are told, lies the key to the plasticity of clay in that it appears to be the size of the clay particle as well as its shape which decides the ease with which a lump of clay can be fashioned and manipulated without falling apart. Before continuing with secondary clays, more about plasticity may be of use as well as of interest.

Plasticity can be simply described as the shaping or fashioning properties of a material. It appears that minerals of small grain size are more plastic than minerals of large grain size. Also where the unit structure is lamellar or scale-like and is almost two-dimensional, the plasticity is greater than where the unit structure is three-dimensional. This explains why minerals such as sand having a three-dimensional structure can never be as plastic as clay which has a two-dimensional structure, no matter how fine the grains are. Clay is therefore minute in grain size and scale-like in structure. When water is added to the clay it surrounds the grains and acts as a lubricant, allowing them to slip around on each other. Cohesion between the grains is maintained by electrical attraction and gravitation. If the water evaporates from the clay the flat-faced grains lose their lubrication and stick together. So the clay becomes hard and non-plastic. Another interesting point can be dealt with here as to why non-plastic materials like sand, while having some modelling properties when wet, collapse on drying out. It is again a question of grain shape. The flat-dimensional grain has much more contact area than the point contact of the three-dimensional grain. Therefore when the water evaporates from the sand the point contact is not sufficient to hold the grains together and the mass collapses.

Secondary clays are therefore plastic, and vary in colour, texture and composition depending on the amounts of free silica, iron, organic matter, lime, etc., which they have picked up in transit. Secondary clays are classified as refractory, vitrifiable or fusible depending on their fusing or softening temperatures when heated.

### Refractory clays

These are clays which are able to withstand high temperatures (1500°C+) without fusing or losing their shape. The most common of the refractories is fireclay which comes from the coal measures. This is the underclay or seatearth on which the coal seam rests and is the ancient soil of the forest from which the coal has been formed. Because it supported plant life for such a long time, the potash and soda compounds (alkalies) have been extracted, leaving only a very small amount of iron or other fluxes. It has therefore a low alkali content and sometimes contains up to 50% free silica. Fireclays are used for making refractory bricks and materials for kiln and furnace linings, saggars and kiln furniture generally. They can also be used, however, as additions to stoneware bodies to give roughness and to reduce shrinkage and warpage. Although fireclays vary in colour and texture, the best are a soft grey colour in the raw state, relatively coarse grained and therefore of moderate plasticity, and fire to a buff colour.

While not nearly so refractory as fireclay, another important clay to come into this group is ball clay. These secondary clays, which are found in Dorset and Devon, are noted for their purity and plasticity. In the raw state they are commonly bluey-grey in colour due to the carbonaceous matter they contain. In the firing this organic matter burns away leaving the pot an off-white colour. Because of their excessive shrinkage they are rarely used alone but are added to other clay bodies to increase plasticity and are extensively used with china clay in the manufacture of white earthenware. The name 'ball' clay appears to have originated in Shelton, Staffordshire, in about 1720, when John Astbury started using this Devonshire clay in the development of a new white ware. For ease in handling in transit from Devonshire to Staffordshire, the clay was made into balls, shipped by sea to the Mersey and then carries by packhorse to Shelton.

### Vitrifiable clays

These are clays which vitrify or become non-porous between 1200°C and 1350°C. Many so-called 'bastard fireclays' would come into this group because their alkalies or flux content makes their refractoriness too low for use in refractory materials. Vitrifiable clays are used for stoneware, building bricks, paving tiles, sanitary ware, terracotta and any pottery requiring a high temperature vitrified body that does not twist or warp.

### Fusible clays

These clays lose their shape at about 1200°C and are the common iron stained 'red' and yellow clays found near the surface in practically all countries. Their firing temperature is generally in the range of 1000°–1100°C and whatever the raw clay colour they almost all fire 'red'-brown.

Notable pieces of English pottery made in this type of clay are the unglazed red 'stonewares' of John and David Elers made at Bradwell Wood, Staffordshire, in the seventeenth century. There is also the Yi-hsing unglazed 'red' stonewares of China, imported into England at about the same time.

# Other pottery bodies

While it is convenient for theory purposes to fit clays into categories, in practice it is not always so simple as no one clay has exactly the same properties as another found in a different site. It is necessary therefore to have other materials in addition to clays, which can be mixed with the clay to improve its refractoriness, density, colour and texture. By adding flint, quartz, sand and grog, the refractory properties of a clay can be improved. Also by adding felspar, Cornish stone and in certain cases lime, the fusion and density properties can be adjusted.

## Felspar

It has been stated that clay is formed as a result of the decomposition of felspar. Felspar is, however, of great importance to the potter in its undecomposed state as a major flux in both clays and glazes.

Felspar is a mineral made up of alumina and silica and the alkali potash or soda, or both. Felspar which contains more potash than soda (potassium felspar) is called orthoclase or microcline and that which contains more soda than potash (sodium felspar) is called albite. Sodium felspar has the greater fluxing power and is often favoured for glazes because of its lower melting-point. Some felspars fuse by themselves at 1140°C in contrast to others which fuse at 1280°C; the average fusing point being about 1250°C.

Pure felspars are not found in England. Norway, Sweden, Russia and the United States are countries having the purest deposits. Nepheline syenite is an American felspar which has an unusually high proportion of sodium and potassium in relation to silica. Consequently, if it is used in clays and glazes instead of other felspars, a much lower maturing temperature can be obtained.

## Cornish stone (china stone, pegmatite)

This is partially decomposed granite having a high percentage of felspar. Mined, as its name suggests, in Cornwall, it is the English source of felspar, since no pure forms are found in this country. Though with slightly less fluxing power it can be used as an alternative to pure felspar in both medium and high temperature clays and glazes.

Cornish stone is similar in characteristics to petuntze, the finely crushed felspathic rock which was the major ingredient in the Chinese porcelain bodies and glazes.

## Whiting

This is calcium carbonate or chalk which, when finely ground, is used for introducing lime into pottery bodies and glazes. It is one of the main fluxes in stoneware and porcelain glazes.

## Flint

This is a hard mineral and a variety of quartz found in chalky areas in pebble form. Noted areas in England being Kent, Essex and the Channel coast beaches. It is almost pure silica and when calcined it can be crushed into powder form for adding to clays and glazes. It is non-plastic and generally thought of as a refractory. When introduced into clay bodies it promotes whiteness and density, reduces shrinkage and helps to prevent warping.

## Quartz

A crystalline form of almost pure silica. When ground to a fine powder it can be used as an alternative to flint, particularly in high temperature pottery.

## Sand

This is a commodity found in natural abundance and can be described as a mass of quartz rock grains usually containing impurities such as iron. Its high silica content makes it another material for introducing this element into clay. It has the properties of making plastic clays short, reducing shrinkage and warpage and produces openness of texture.

Potters' merchants have stocks of sand graded in grain size and colour. Silver sand is the purest and is supplied in fine powder form.

This fine sand is of particular use as a placing material in kiln packing. However, it may well be worth experimenting with ordinary builders' sand and sea sand.

## Grog

This is pot (generally speaking, fired fireclay) which has been crushed for the purpose of introducing into clay bodies to aid drying, reduce shrinkage and warpage, and produce openness of texture.

Grog is available from potters' merchants in a variety of grain sizes ranging from extra coarse, which will not pass a 20-mesh sieve, to very fine which will pass through a 60-mesh sieve. (As a suggestion, the 40–60 mesh is a good starter.) The nature of the grogged clay is therefore governed by the mesh size of the grog which can be added in quantities of usually up to 20% grog to clay.

### Bentonite

This is a natural colloidal clay of extreme plasticity. Imported from America, this clay has been formed by the weathering of volcanic ash and is found as calcium bentonite in Wyoming and sodium bentonite in Mississippi. Used mainly for making short clays plastic in proportions of up to 4%, it is about five times more effective than ball clay. It is also very useful for holding glaze particles in suspension thus preventing them settling into a stiff mass at the bottom of the container. In proportions of up to 2%, this should prevent much irritation and time-wasting labour.

### Bone ash

This is animal bones (predominantly those of oxen) which have been calcined and then crushed to a fine powder. When mixed with china clay and felspar or Cornish stone in proportions of 30–50%, it is instrumental in producing the translucency which is so characteristic of English bone china.

# The preparation of clay

From the description of clay, its properties and additives, it will be appreciated that one can dig, blend and make adjustments to clay in order to produce a specific body for a specific job. Digging one's own clay is an important and interesting exercise in many ways. For example, it widens one's geological knowledge of a local environment, develops experience in clay preparation and increases the possibility of producing new effects in the finished ware – an ambition of every artist. It is also useful as an occasional group activity for children and students engaged in pottery-making. As a permanent venture, however, it usually proves to be quite impractical, as well as impossible, for several reasons. Time is an important factor to most people and digging clay and then preparing and testing it is very time-consuming even if one is lucky enough to find a suitable, accessible deposit close at hand. While clay of one sort or another can be found in most localities, it is not always possible to get at. Also, while one is searching for, digging and preparing clay, pots are not being produced. Therefore as the raw materials for preparing specific clay bodies and glazes have to be purchased from the potters' merchant anyway, it is convenient and often inevitable that the prepared clays should come from them as well. Potclays Ltd supply a wide variety of prepared clays and I have included their address along with the names and addresses of other merchants at the back of this book.

## Preparing local clay

When embarking on a clay-finding mission, a start may be made by obtaining a Regional Geology of Great Britain Handbook of your area from one of HM Stationery Offices. This will provide information about local clay deposits. A visit to a local brickworks should also prove helpful, with information on both clay and deposits.

As surface clay is usually mixed with too much soil or humus, it is by and large unsatisfactory for pottery purposes. One must therefore prospect for deeper exposed seams such as in building excavations or road cuttings. On the north-east coast of England we are fortunate in having an abundant supply of boulder clay forming much of the cliff face. This clay deposit was formed by glacial transportation during the Great Ice Age when ice advanced from the Lake District and the Cheviots. It is easily accessible in the cliffs of the east coast and is of good plasticity due not only to its glacial milling but also to the continued weathering it receives – a condition which all newly dug clays must be subjected to if they are to mature properly.

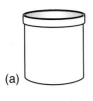

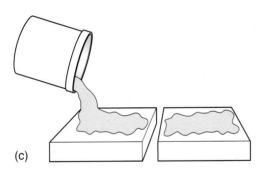

■ Fig. 1. The preparation of plastic clay from slip: (a) Broken up clay in a container; (b) Passing slip through 60–80 mesh sieve; (c) Running slip onto plaster slab for drying.

No matter from where the clay is dug, the procedure for its preparation will be the same and is as follows:

1  The freshly dug clay should be left in heaps exposed to sun, rain and frost for a period of one to two years. This is so that the clay particles can be broken down still further, resulting in a more plastic and workable body. The heaps of clay should be turned every few months to ensure uniform weathering. However, I should say at this point that the boulder clay I have used has never had a weathering period except for its time on the cliff face. This

must have obviously been enough, as the pots made from it were satisfactory, with little shrinkage. Biscuit-fired at 1120°C, the thin coat of glaze fired at 1060°C proved craze resistant. Maybe this was luck but all pottery needs a certain amount – no matter how sophisticated the manufacture of it.

It is a fact that clay, like wine, improves with keeping, and clays in the Dorset workings are weathered for three years before they are used. I do therefore suggest that the clay be weathered as long as possible before use.

2  Remove as much débris as possible – pebbles, leaves, etc. – and put the broken-up clay into a suitably-sized container (Fig. 1(a)); a wooden barrel is excellent for this purpose together with a bucket for test samples, but a galvanized or plastic dustbin is equally useful. Add water to the clay and, with a paddle or stick, stir the mixture into a cream-like consistency. This is called slip.

3  Pass the slip through a 60–80 mesh sieve to remove the remaining coarse impurities (Fig. 1(b)). Finer sieving will remove sand particles necessary in the prevention of excessive shrinkage. The slip can be collected in another vessel of comparable size and the sediment allowed to settle.

4  Drain the surplus water from the thickened solution and run the thick slip on to plaster of Paris slabs for drying into a workable plastic state (Fig. 1(c)). Plaster of Paris slabs are the most effective way of drying slip clay out as the plaster is relatively cheap, available from most builders' merchants, will cast into almost any size and shape and when dry is extremely absorbent.

The clay, when dry to a plastic state, is ready for the final stages of preparation, namely wedging and kneading. These processes should be carried out with purchased clay as well as home-prepared clay, primarily to remove pockets of air from the mass. Air bubbles are detrimental to the working properties of the clay and to the finished results.

## Wedging

This is the hand method of mixing plastic clay into a de-aired homo-genous mass. It is used for preparing clay that has dried out on the plaster slab, mixing two

■ Fig. 2. Clay ready for cutting.

■ Fig. 3. Cutting clay.

clays of different plastic consistency, blending two different coloured clays together (although this is better done in the slip form), and introducing sand and grog into a body.

The technique, while seeming to be clumsy and disorganized, is in fact a systematic procedure to ensure that the mass receives uniform treatment. It is as follows:

1   Make sure that you have a strong table or bench, topped with either a slab of marble or slate on which to work. A slab of plaster will do for very soft sticky clay. A non-absorbent surface will cause the clay to stick to it.

2   Beat the plastic clay into a slab-shaped lump which can be lifted easily.

3   Pick up the lump and drop it on its end so that the mass is self-supporting and at an angle of approximately 45° to the work surface (Fig. 2).

4   Using an 18 in. (457 mm) length of stainless steel or brass wire with dowelled ends, cut upwards through the mass at approximately 45° (Fig. 3). (Two lengths of 24-gauge wire twisted together will give extra strength.)

■ Fig. 4. Raising the cut piece

5   Holding the top half of the mass in both hands, raise it above the head and bring it down hard, reverse side, on to the ridge of the lower lump. Both cut edges should now be facing you (Figs. 4 and 5).

6   Press the mass into a slab form again, working from the centre outwards with the flat and heel of the hand to dispel the air. Pat round the edges of the mass to keep it a tidy and manageable lump.

7   Lift the lump up and turn it over and then, turning it in a quarter circle, drop it on its end again at an angle of 45°. The whole process is then repeated until it is decided that the clay is of a satisfactory consistency and blend for its final de-airing.

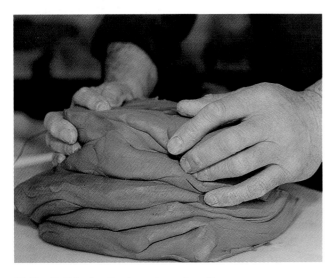

■ Fig. 5. Bringing the two pieces together.

## Kneading

This is the hand method of removing any remaining air from the plastic clay after the wedging process and is the clay's final preparation before being fashioned. There are two variations of kneading. One is known as ram's or bull's head kneading, because of the shape of the kneaded clay. The other is known as spiral kneading because of the spiral section of the kneaded clay. This latter method, used by oriental potters, is suitable for preparing both small and very large lumps of clay.

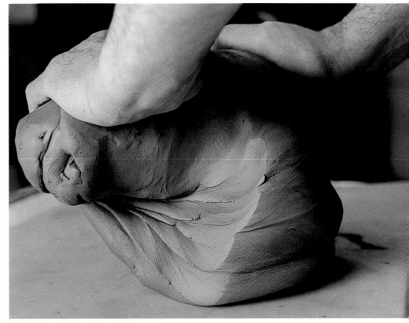

■ Fig. 6. Ram's head kneading.

Both methods cause the clay mass to be 'folded' over and over thus squashing all the remaining air out of the lump and are carried out as follows:

### Ram's head kneading

1   Take a piece of wedged clay of manageable size and beat it into a block shape on the working surface.

2   With the hands gripping the sides of the block, press forward, forcing the heel of the hands into the mass of clay.

3   Roll the clay back and press forward again, directing the force of the hands slightly towards the centre of the mass. This latter action keeps the clay in a controllable form (Fig. 6).

4   This repeat action is continued until it is decided that the clay is air free (perhaps 5–10 mins).

### Spiral kneading

**1**  Block a piece of wedged clay on the working surface.

**2**  Place the block on its end and grip the top end with both hands.

**3**  Force the heel of the right or left hand towards the centre of the mass.

**4**  Then, with the other hand, pull the clay back on its heel and give it a slight turn (clockwise if pulling it back with the left hand or anti-clockwise if pulling it back with the right). The ridge caused by the pressure of the first hand movement should now be facing you.

**5**  Repeat the movements as in Steps 3 and 4, pressing into the ridge of the mass with one hand and then pulling the clay back around with the other (Fig. 7). Again, this process is repeated until it is decided that the clay is air free. However, care must be taken not to over-prepare the clay. Remember that while the clay is being wedged and kneaded, it is drying out, due not only to the absorbency of the working surface, but also to heat from the hands. Therefore, as soon as the clay feels to be of a suitable working consistency, cut through the mass with a wire and check the section. If it appears to be air free and well blended, wrap the clay tightly in polythene until it is needed. This will prevent further loss of moisture.

## Preparing blended clays

In addition to digging one's own clay, buying prepared plastic clay and introducing sand, grog, etc. into both, one can prepare earthenware and porcelain bodies from powdered raw materials supplied by the potters' merchant. The clays are compounded by carefully weighing out the ingredients in the listed proportions and mixing the dry compound with water in an approximate ratio of 1 kilogram to 1 litre of water (2 lbs to 2 pints approx). The solution can be mixed in a suitable container or in a mechanical blunger supplied by the potters' merchant. The preparation is then the same as already described with the exception that the slip is passed through a 100 mesh rather than a 60–80 mesh sieve in order to obtain a more uniform body.

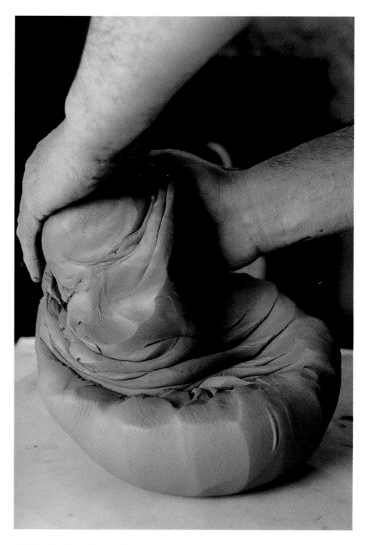

■ Fig. 7. Spiral kneading.

Some typical recipes for the specified bodies are as follows:

### Earthenware body

|  | % (by weight) |
| --- | --- |
| Ball clay | 30 |
| China clay | 24 |
| Flint or quartz | 30 |
| Cornish stone | 16 |

Firing temperature approximately 1120°C.

## Stoneware body

|  | % (by weight) |
|---|---|
| Stoneware clay | 40 |
| Fireclay | 20 |
| Ball clay | 20 |
| Cornish stone | 10 |
| Flint or quartz | 5 |
| Grog (60 mesh) | 5 |

Firing temperature approximately 1250°C.

If natural stoneware clay is not available, china clay and ball clay could take its place. A small quantity of iron oxide or red clay would make the fired clay darker and perhaps more interesting. An alternative stoneware recipe would therefore read:

|  | % (by weight) |
|---|---|
| China clay | 40 |
| Ball clay | 30 |
| Flint or quartz | 10 |
| Cornish stone | 10 |
| Iron oxide or red clay | 5 |
| Grog (60 mesh) | 5 |

Firing temperature approximately 1250°C.

In both stoneware recipes I have included a small percentage of grog because, in my experience, stoneware clays without this or sand have a tendency to excessive shrinkage and warpage, particularly on things like coffee-pot necks, where measurement and symmetry are of great importance. The degree of texture is a matter of choice and depends of course on the quantity of grog used and its grain size. A 60-mesh grog is perhaps the best starter, and this is added after the other materials have been sieved.

## Porcelain body

Porcelain bodies, or 'pastes' as they are known, are generally a mixture of china clay and felspar or Cornish stone. However, to make this mixture plastic enough to work, ball clay is added. Therefore a typical recipe for this type of body would read:

|  | % (by weight) |
|---|---|
| China clay | 45 |
| Felspar or Cornish stone | 30 |
| Ball clay | 10 |
| Flint or quartz | 15 |

Firing temperature approximately 1250°C.

If a more plastic clay is required, 2–3% bentonite may be used to make up the 10% ball clay, remembering that bentonite has a high shrinkage rate and must therefore be used sparingly.

If the body is still difficult to work, the ball clay may be increased and the china clay decreased. This of course will reduce the body's translucency.

## Bone china body

This porcelain body has bone ash in addition to the china clay and felspar or Cornish stone. In combination with the felspar this is a powerful flux and produces a highly translucent body. A starting recipe for this type of body would be:

|  | % (by weight) |
|---|---|
| China clay | 25 |
| Felspar or Cornish stone | 30 |
| Bone ash | 45 |

Firing temperature approximately 1240°C.

Bone china bodies are not suitable for throwing but are fashioned by the jolley and casting methods. The slight plasticity of natural bone ash makes them workable by these methods without the addition of ball clay.

# The preparation of slips for casting and decoration

## Casting slip

In a slip used for casting, the amount of water required to make the dry materials fluid is considerably reduced by the addition of a very small quantity of deflocculant. The deflocculant is a combination of the alkalies sodium silicate (water glass) and sodium carbonate (soda ash). Sodium silicate is supplied in two densities measured in °TW (degrees Twadell). These densities are 75°TW and 140°TW, the former being the thinner solution, and more generally used in the less plastic porcelain and china-clay slips. While sodium silicate can be used alone as a deflocculant, it is much more efficient in combination with sodium carbonate.

The simple explanation of the action which takes place is that the electrical forces present in the alkaline solution cause repulsion in the clay particles, thus dispersing them. Too much deflocculant, however, causes the reverse action and the slip will become stiff once more.

The advantages of deflocculated slip for casting are mainly due to the reduced water content in that the casts are denser, dry quicker and shrink and warp less. The excess slip also drains cleanly from the cast and the cast is more easily released from the mould.

The prepared slip should have a pint weight of 34–36 oz (litre weight of 2000 grammes approx). If the slip is any denser it will be insufficiently fluid. If the slip is less dense the casts will be flabby with excessive shrinkage and warpage and the moulds will become quickly saturated. Therefore a starter recipe for a casting slip would read:

| | % (by weight) |
|---|---|
| Powdered body | 100 |
| + | |
| Sodium silicate | 0.2 – 0.3 |
| Soda ash | 0.2 – 0.3 |
| Water | 40 |

## Mixing the slip

1 Dissolve the deflocculants in a small quantity of hot water.
2 Put this solution with the measured amount of water in a suitable container.
3 Add the powdered body in small quantities stirring all the time (a blunger or a special electric mixer would be an invaluable asset here).
4 Put the slip through an 80-mesh sieve and cover the container, otherwise a skin may form on the top of the slip and reduce its pouring qualities.

Another way of preparing casting slips, suitable for beginners, is to take 100 parts of very soft plastic body and add the deflocculant solution to this, adding water sparingly, if necessary.

## Correcting faults in the casting slip

1 If the slip casts slowly and the results are dense and brittle, try using less deflocculant.
2 If the slip casts too quickly and the results are flabby, try using more deflocculant.
3 If the slip casts correctly but is too thick and sticky to pour from the mould, try adding more water.

## Slips or engobes for decoration

An engobe is another name for a slip which is applied to a form made from plastic body either to provide contrast in colour or to change the colour of the form entirely. The methods of decorating with engobes will be described more fully at a later stage. At this point, however, it is necessary to know how to prepare and colour engobes and the properties an engobe must have if it is to be of any use for decoration.

The aims in mixing an engobe are:

- To give a suitably dense coating to the ware in required colours.
- To secure a successful fit between engobe and plastic body so that the engobe does not peel or flake off the ware due to different shrinkage rates in drying out and firing.
- To mature at a similar temperature to the body from which the ware is made.
- To take a glaze without pulling away from the ware.

These conditions are easily satisfied if the engobe is made basically from the ware plastic body and is applied while the ware is still damp. Engobes may also be applied to the ware when it has dried out or has been biscuit-fired. These engobes are made up from china clay and ball clay for whiteness, varying amounts of flint and calcined china clay to reduce shrinkage, and felspar or leadless frit as a flux to help adhesion. The problems when applying slip at these stages of maturation are, of course, counteracting the different shrinkage rates. Therefore, as the decoration possibilities and the ease of application strongly favour the damp stage application, I am not including recipes for adjusted slips. For more information refer to Daniel Rhodes' *Clay and Glazes for the Potter* (see Taking it further).

The recipes given for the preparation of plastic bodies would do very well as basic slips. Alternatively, powdered white and red bodies purchased from a supplier work well. Then, by use of a white body for light colours and a red body for dark colours, the slips can be stained by adding metal oxides or stains in the following proportions:

| Using 100% white body + | | Using 100% red body + | |
| --- | --- | --- | --- |
| 2% Cobalt oxide | blue | 2% cobalt oxide | black |
| 3% Copper oxide | green | + 3% iron oxide | black |
| 6% Iron oxide | tan | + 2% manganese oxide | black |
| 8% Vanadium stain | yellow | 100% powered red body | brown |

If a very white basic slip is required, two recipes which I often use for their simplicity in mixing as well as their whiteness, are as follows:

- China clay    50%
- Ball clay    50%

- China clay    45%
- Ball clay    45%
- Flint    10%

The above list is intended just as a starter guide. Oxides can be added to the basic slips with safety in quantities of up to 10%, and stains in quantities of up to 15%, giving a wide range of colour.

The slips are, of course, prepared in the same way as previously described. The oxides and stains should first be mixed with a small quantity of water and then added to the slip. The whole is then passed through an 80–100 mesh sieve. This should allow the slip colour to remain slightly speckled. If this is not considered to give added beauty then, of course, the slip must be sieved through a finer mesh.

# Testing new slips and clays

It may seem rather a chore to make tests on clays but this may save much time and frustration in the long run.

Bought slips and clays are usually reliable. However, on rare occasions I have been sent faulty batches of both clay and pigments. I did not bother to test them and while these were replaced free of charge, no compensation could be made for the frustration at the loss of valued work. On one occasion, a whole kiln full of stoneware completely collapsed because of a factory error. An operative had used china stone instead of china clay in the mix, and what should have been a stoneware body was in fact a badly formulated stoneware 'glaze'.

With locally dug and self-prepared clays, testing is essential in order to assess shrinkage, strength and working properties. While test pieces may take a variety of forms, I think it is better to make small useful shapes rather than small lumps or rolls out of the body. For example, small unturned bowls made on a wheel always have a use and are ideal for testing the throwing properties of a clay as well as those of shrinkage, strength and ability to take a glaze. Assuming of course that the clay is successfully tested, rolls of the material are useless for anything but reference. However, a quick test of a clay's plasticity is to make a thin roll out of the body and bend it. If it cracks or breaks, the clay is not very plastic and consequently will have relatively poor working qualities, particularly on the wheel.

# Storage of ceramic materials

Storing materials, which amounts to keeping them in good condition until they are required, is a chore which must be done if time and money are not to be wasted unnecessarily. Materials should be kept in a suitably covered container and *properly labelled*. This will preserve them and prevent one from being mistaken for another, as many ceramic materials look alike in the raw state. Some materials, like metal oxides, are potentially toxic if mishandled and careless storage can become a health hazard. Dust is another health hazard which should be controlled carefully.

## Storing plastic clay

The aim when storing plastic clay is to keep it in a suitable working condition, i.e. moist.

Plastic clay, as supplied by the potters' merchant, is conveniently sent in polythene bags or wrappers and will keep for a long time without any attention, so long as the wrapper is not punctured. Reclaimed and self-prepared clay may be preserved in the same way, as this is a cleaner and more efficient method than the often recommended damp cloth methods. Polythene, if properly used, provides an airtight cover preventing the odour which sometimes accompanies the decaying organic matter in clay which has been stored for some time. It also has the advantage of not rotting, which is an annoying characteristic of damp cloth or hessian, especially when the fibres become entangled with the clay.

Plastic dustbins with tight-fitting lids are efficient for clay storage and are preferable to the traditional galvanized ones in that they are lighter to move about. However, they can crack if roughly handled or overloaded.

For larger quantities of clay it may be necessary to construct large box-like containers with brick walls, detachable wooden fronts, tight-fitting lids and zinc-lined interiors (Fig. 8(d)). These, however, would be a permanent fixture and thought would have to be given to their siting if they were not to become a cumbersome waste of space.

Whatever method of storage is used the clay should be inspected from time to time and if found to be in danger of drying out, should be thoroughly doused with water and recovered. I have found that in my studio, and particularly in the classroom, clay stays in storage for such a short time that it requires very little attention before use.

## Storing slip clay

Slip clay may be stored in polythene containers with tight-fitting snap-on or screw-top lids. These containers may be purchased in different shapes and sizes and, while not cheap, save much time, labour and mess. There might be a local supplier, which would cut costs. For example, I have found that the local 'Brew-it-Yourself' shop sells a relatively cheap but good quality plastic bucket with a snap-on lid. A saving may also be made by collecting discarded plastic vegetable oil, salt and vinegar containers. A thorough wash, and these containers are usually as good as new. Whatever the container it should be airtight.

The slip should be shaken or stirred from time to time to prevent it settling into an unworkable mass. It should also be sieved each time before being used to remove any lumps which have formed in storage or dry flakes which inevitably cluster around the neck of the container and fall into the slip when the lid is removed.

## Storing other ceramic materials

Most ceramic materials are supplied in powder form in paper-lined hessian sacks, polythene bags or paper packs. When the sack or packet is opened, it then becomes an inefficient means of storage and sometimes a health risk. It is better, therefore, to store the materials that are in use in strong containers with tight-fitting lids. Remember to label the containers, preferably with a waterproof marker, as stick-on tags fall off. It is also better to keep the same container for the same materials when re-stocking.

# Reclaiming dry, unworkable or used clay

In addition to having bins for storing plastic clay it is necessary to have them for reclaiming used and dry clay. This clay should be broken into small pieces, dropped into the bin and covered with water (Fig. 8(a)). When the clay has softened, excess water should be skimmed off and the soggy mass spread on to plaster slabs to dry out (Fig. 8(b)). When the clay is suitably plastic, it can be put through the pugmill (see Fig. 8(c) and glossary), wedged and kneaded.

The number of bins required for reclaiming clays obviously depends on the number of clays being used.

A different bin is needed for each clay and it is best to label them. I usually have four bins, containing a general-purpose earthenware-stoneware buff body, a red body, a grogged stoneware body and a mixture of odds and ends for sculptural pottery, tiles, etc.

# Making a plaster slab

Plaster slabs are essential for drying out slip or soggy clay into a more plastic body. Also, when a slate or marble-topped bench is not available, one topped in plaster would be ideal for wedging and kneading sticky clay and drying out the clay as well.

Plaster of Paris is relatively cheap, easy to mix and in the wet stage will follow any shape of mould. When properly mixed with water it forms a hard dry substance of high porosity which will absorb and release moisture quickly. This quality, which makes it the essential material for slip casting, will be discussed at a later stage.

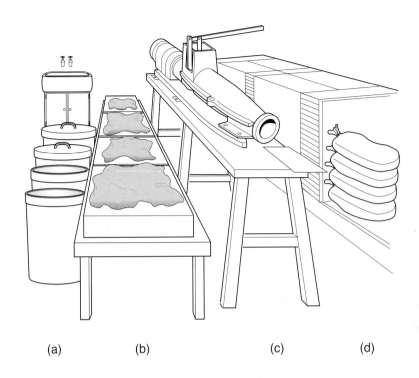

(a)          (b)          (c)          (d)

■ Fig. 8. Plant for reclaiming, preparing and storing clay. (a) Bins for reclaiming clay; (b) Plastic slabs for drying out wet clay; (c) Pugmill for mixing plastic clay; (d) storage boxes.

The number and size of slabs required will, of course, depend on space, movability and the quantity of clay to be prepared. A useful size as a starter would be 60 cm × 60 cm × 10 cm (2 ft × 2 ft × 4 in.), and this would be cast in the following way:

1  Arrange four wooden boards 71 cm × 71 cm × 15 cm × 1.5 cm (2⅓ ft × 2⅓ ft × 6 in. × ½ in. approx) in a box formation on a flat surface which has been coated thoroughly with potters' size. An angle iron on the corner of each board will allow them to be arranged in numerous sizes up to 71 cm × 71 cm × 15 cm and will hold them firmly in place.

2  All joints, the base and corners, are then sealed with clay to stop the plaster from leaking out.

**3**  Half fill a large plastic bowl with water and lightly sprinkle the plaster over its surface, preferably through a coarse sieve to remove lumps (Fig. 9(a)). Do not drop handfuls in at a time. Do this until the water will absorb no more and the plaster begins to build up on the surface. This is called 'saturation point'. Perhaps a more accurate water to plaster measurement is a ratio of 1.5 lb plaster to 1 pt water (681 gm to 568 ml).

**4**  Leave the mix for about a minute so that the plaster can become thoroughly saturated. Then stir the mixture for about two minutes until it becomes a creamy solution without lumps. A hand is the best stirring instrument because fingers will seek out any lumps whereas other aids will not.

**5**  Pour the solution quickly into the mould taking care not to trap air in the corners. Tap the mould to make sure that any trapped air comes to the surface and the top levels off (Fig 9(b)).

**6**  One mixing may not be sufficient. The surface must therefore be scored or 'teased' as the plaster sets to form a key for the next pouring. When the half-way stage is reached a flat piece of chicken wire, cut slightly smaller than the mould, can be pressed on to the plaster to give reinforcement to the slab.

**7**  Subsequent pouring should be carried out as the first one, tapping the mould to de-air and level off the plaster.

**8**  The plaster may become warm to the touch as it hardens off which is a good indication that it is active. Finally, when the plaster has set hard, the mould can be removed and any untidy edges bevelled with a plaster or surform plane (Fig 9(c)). This helps to prevent the edges chipping and getting into the clay. It also gives the slab a finished and tidy appearance. The slab can now be put into a warm place to really dry out. It may be a week before the slab is ready for use.

In addition to the mixing of plaster, there are one or two other points which must be noted if the material is to be an aid rather than a handicap. These are:

■  Do not pour surplus plaster down the drain. This will set and eventually cause a blockage which can be very expensive to put right. Pour it on to a piece of newspaper and when set, simply fold up the

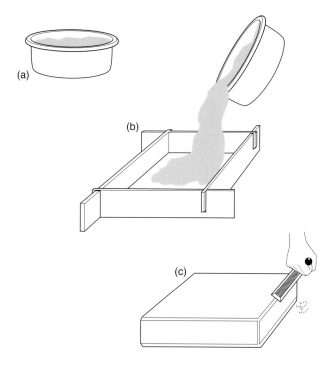

■ Fig. 9. Making a plaster slab. (a) The bowl of mixed plaster; (b) Pouring the plaster into the mould; (c) Bevelling the edges of the plaster block.

paper for disposal. I always keep small cardboard boxes handy for surplus plaster. The resulting plaster blocks are very useful for the children to carve.

■  Always test a batch of plaster before use to make sure that it is active.

■  Once stirring has begun, no more plaster should be added to the mixture to thicken it, nor water added to thin it down.

■  When cleaning dried clay from the plaster slab use a flat blunt scraper made of hardboard or wood. This should avoid any plaster being scraped up with the clay. Plaster in clay can cause holes to blow out in fired ware and bits of glaze to fall off the pot sometimes months after the ware has been finished.

■  Plaster should be stored in a bin, clearly labelled, with a tight-fitting lid. The plaster will then remain dry and active.

# 3

# Methods of working clay

## Thumb or pinch shapes

'Pinching' is undoubtedly one of the most primitive methods of shaping clay into an intended form. Requiring no tools, except fingers, the method readily lends itself to the imitation of fruit and vegetable forms, these being the food and water containers of early man. Not only will the method allow the fashioning of a bowl shape with some aesthetic appeal, but will also provide a foundation for model making and pottery sculpture. Indeed, 'pinching' has become a standard procedure for introducing clay work to beginners both young and old. It breaks the novice in gently to the manipulative skills required for working the material, popularly known as 'getting the feel of the clay'. It also gives an indication of the material's qualities and failings. However. 'pinching' should not be looked upon solely as a beginners' exercise for, within its apparent limitations, many beautiful pots are made.

While I have seen teapots made using the pinch method, this is rather a laboured use of the technique; the natural development is in the bowl range of forms. The basic procedure for this type of shape is as follows:

1   Take a prepared lump of plastic clay and knock it into the size and shape of a tennis ball.
2   Hold the ball of clay in one hand and press the thumb of the other hand into the centre of the ball. Leave enough clay beneath the thumb from which to fashion the base.
3   Slowly rotate the ball of clay in one hand and repeatedly pinch the walls of the clay with the thumb and first finger of the other, starting at the base and working slowly towards the outer rim (Fig. 10). This will quickly cause the ball to become a chunky bowl shape of even thickness throughout.
4   The procedure is then simply repeated until the aims of form and thickness are achieved (Fig. 11). Remember to keep your hands damp while working the clay otherwise it will soon become unworkable and begin to crack. A wet, flat sponge on the table is ideal for keeping hands moist.

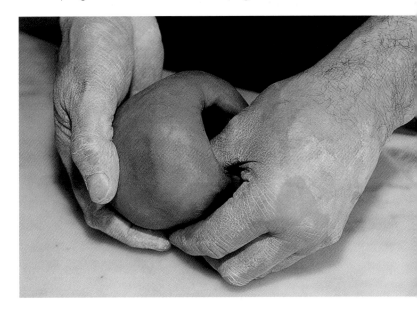

■ Fig. 10. Opening out the form from a ball of clay.

**pottery**

■ Fig. 11. Completing the form.

The pinched bowl can be made stable by lightly tapping the base on the working surface. If it is thought that a footring would improve the appearance of this very simple form, one can easily be pinched out of the base. The base should obviously be thick enough to support the form in the firing. If, however, there is insufficient clay at the base to pinch a footring, a ringed roll of clay may be attached and the footring pinched from this. Attaching one piece of clay to another is generally done by roughening or 'teasing' the surfaces to be joined, painting them lightly with slip made from the same clay, pressing them firmly together and finally smoothing the exposed edges with a finger or modelling tool.

The type of finish to give the pinched form, as with any other ware, is of course for the potter to decide. I would suggest, however, that not using some of the natural textures created by the different methods of

working clay would seem to defeat the purpose of having different methods in the first place. For example, in the case of a pinched form, some of the pinch marks may enhance the form and it would be a pity to completely smooth them out. A smooth surface, if required, can be achieved by smoothing across the clay with a vertical, horizontal and diagonal motion, first with the finger and then with a metal scraper. Burnishing the surface is another finish for thumb shapes (Fig. 12) but this will be explained in the section on decoration later in the book.

In addition to making bowl forms, pinching is a useful method for making pottery sculpture. Whether realistic or abstract, the form can be fashioned out of a single piece of clay eliminating the need for joins. This is particularly useful when working with children as the animal model is restricted to the size of the clay lump and does not develop into yards of body without a head (see opposite). Of course clay may be added if required.

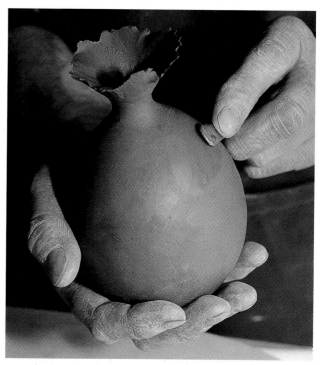

■ Fig. 12. Burnishing the surface.

■ A variety of coiled shapes.

# Coiled shapes

'Coiling' is another hand method of building hollow form in clay. Used in societies before the invention of the potter's wheel, and in places where the wheel has never been introduced, the coiling method is now used by studio potters in pursuit of large pure form rather than functional ware. Coiling is still the main method of making vessels in primitive societies such as the Hottentots of South-West Africa, the BaGanda of East Africa and on the Oceanic Islands such as the New Hebrides. In Britain the first coil pottery appears to be attributed to the Food Vessel Folk of Northumberland who were a partially nomadic people living in the Early Bronze Age (1700–1300 BC). The most characteristic features of their pots are the impressed herring-bone and zig-zag motifs.

## Making a hollow coiled form

As a possible development of the pinch method for making larger forms, coiling is perhaps the next stage in developing the manipulative skills of the beginner. The method is as follows:

1   Take a piece of prepared plastic clay, roll it into a ball shape then flatten this on the bench top with the heel of the hand. The resulting disc shape is the base of the vessel. A flatter larger disc may be made with the help of a rolling pin, imperfections in the symmetry of the disc being trimmed off with a flat blade (Fig. 13). The amount of clay used for the base is, of course, relative to the size and shape of the proposed vessel. The base can now be put on to a whirler or banding wheel, a flat board, or just left on the bench top. The point to remember is that the shape must be frequently turned during its construction to check the evenness of the form.

2   Take another handful of clay and squeeze it into a rough cylinder shape. Place this cylinder along the dampened bench top and begin rolling it backwards and forwards under flat hands. Roll the ends of the cylinder first and then, with both hands in the centre, roll out towards the ends. Repeat this procedure until the clay is of a long, round, even, roll section, with an average diameter of about ½ in. (12.70 mm), (Fig 14). Larger pots need bigger rolls.

■ Fig. 13. Making the base with the aid of a templet.

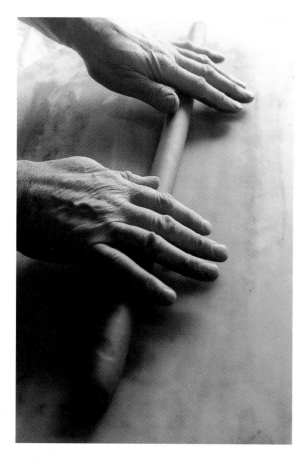

■ Fig. 14. Making long rolls of clay.

**3**  Take the roll of clay and coil it once immediately above the outer edge of the base disc. Overlap the two ends and press the top overlap down into the underneath coil, nipping off the surplus clay in one movement (Fig 15).

**4**  Make another roll of clay as necessary. Then, beginning with the join on the opposite side to the first one, place a second coil directly above the first one and join the ends together as before.

**5**  The two coils and the base should now be 'welded' together by smoothing the clay in a downward direction with the finger on both the inside and outside of the vessel.

**6**  For cylinder shapes the procedure may be repeated as described, beginning with the join on the opposite side to the previous one for added strength and to help keep the top horizontal. I also find that, after smoothing the first

■ Fig. 15. Applying the first coil to the base.

two coils together, it is better to smooth each subsequent coil as it is attached. This gives better control of the overall shape.

If the direction of the form is required to fill out from the vertical line of the cylinder, simply place each subsequent coil slightly towards the outside of the previous one. To bring the form back in again, just reverse this procedure. Therefore by interchanging vertical and diagonal coiling the form can be manipulated at will. A few points to note when coiling are:

■  Always keep your hands damp when working the clay.

- Remember it is the top of the bench which shapes the roll of clay. The hands provide light pressure and motivation. Too much pressure and an incomplete revolution of the rolling action will make an uneven, twisted, flat roll of clay.
- Thumb pressure on the inside of the form, combined with the pinching technique, will give a more even section and cause the shape to fill out slightly from the vertical without any change in direction of the coil.
- Bulbous forms will require support after the initial stages of coiling to prevent them sagging and collapsing. This support can be given with a fat coil of clay and by setting the form into a bowl of sand. Polythene or cloth can cover the sand to prevent it sticking to the clay.
- Lightly beating the top rim and sides of the form with a flat piece of wood will help to keep the top level, force the coils together and give better control of the shape.
- As experience is gained, coiling for large forms may be done fairly quickly with the use of flattened rolls.
- A circular coiled form can be changed into an oval form by gently beating the vessel walls with a flat piece of wood. The finish given to the form is again a matter of taste. The surface can be smoothed down with the fingers, further smoothed with a kidney scraper, using the horizontal-vertical motion, sponged or perhaps burnished. Finger indentations may be left or partially scraped over. Parts of the exterior coil surface may be left unsmoothed and even the whole of it, so long as the coils are thoroughly pressed together and welded on the interior (Fig. 16).

■ Fig. 16. Finishing off the form.

■ Thrown stoneware bowls.

# Thrown shapes

Throwing forms on the potter's wheel has been the most important method of making clay vessels since the wheel's first known origin in Central Asia around 3000 BC. While there are different ways of powering the wheel, the technique of throwing has changed little over the years. The wheel rotates the clay while the potter's hands squeeze, thin and force the clay into the required form. Even in modern industry, with the exception of casting, the basic principles of the wheel are still used. However, the skilful hands of the potter have been replaced by a metal profile and plaster mould of the jigger and jolley machines.

To the studio potter the wheel is of prime importance and I am sure that the satisfaction experienced by those who master the technique of throwing is never matched by any other method of making clay vessels. The technique is direct, spontaneous and crisp, giving pleasure to the spectator as well as to the participant.

## The potter's wheel

While there are various designs of wheel on the market and a variety of plans for building one's own machine, they are all of either the power or kick-wheel type. The kick wheel is operated by a foot treadle mechanism while the power wheel has an electric motor and clutch system. A wheel like the one illustrated (Fig. 17) has given me very good service and is easy to maintain. The advantages of the power wheel are obvious. The kick wheel, however, is cheaper to buy, cheaper to run and is not affected by power cuts.

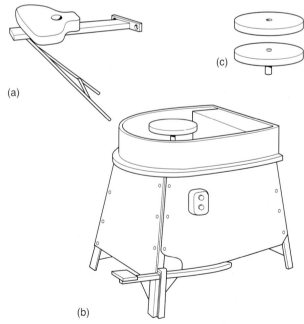

■ Fig. 17. The power wheel. (a) Detachable seat; (b) The wheel; (c) Detachable wheelhead showing bat fitting.

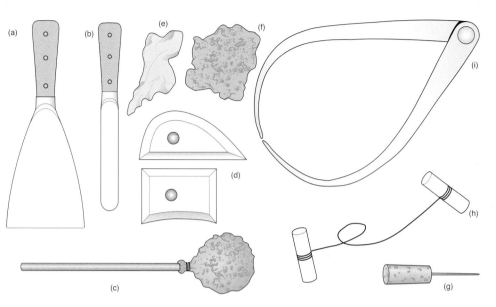

1. Take a piece of prepared plastic clay about the size and shape of a tennis ball and drop it firmly on to the dampened wheel head as near to the centre as possible.
2. Set the wheel in motion and lubricate hands and clay with water.
3. Throwing is carried out in a series of stages. The first of these is called centring. This means pushing or pulling the ball of clay into the centre of the wheel so that it does not wobble from side to side. As the wheel revolves at maximum speed, press down on the clay with the edge of the right hand and push the clay firmly towards the centre of the wheel with the heel of the left hand. If you try to push the clay off the wheel, it will be centred before this happens, so long as the clay has been firmly attached in the first place.

Another way of centring is to grip the clay at the back with both hands and with thumbs resting on top of the lump, pull the clay towards the centre of the wheel (Fig 19). The clay may now be 'worked' a little. Nip it with the heels of both hands so that is is forced up into a column and then take it down again by gripping the clay at the front and

■ Fig. 18. Tools used in throwing. (a) Scraper; (b) Palette knife; (c) Sponge on a stick; (d) Throwing ribs; (e) Piece of chamois leather; (f) Small, natural sponge; (g) Needle set into a cork; (h) Cutting wire; (i) Callipers.

Purchasing a wheel, as any machine, is a matter of taste as well as requirement. Browse through the suppliers' catalogues by all means but, if possible, try out a sample machine before taking the plunge.

## Tools used in throwing

Before starting to throw, check that the tools illustrated in Fig. 18 are available on the tool tray at the back of the wheel.

## Throwing the basic cylinder

When learning to throw, the one shape which must be mastered is the basic cylinder. It is from this shape that most other thrown shapes are developed. The procedure is as follows:

■ Fig. 19. Centring the clay.

applying pressure from the top with the flats of the thumbs. This repeated working up and down of the clay is known as 'coning' and is part of the centring process (Fig. 20). It should force out any remaining air bubbles and render the clay into an ideal condition for the remainder of the throwing process.

Very large lumps of clay may be centred a stage at a time beginning at the top of the lump and working down it.

■ Fig. 20. Coning.

Remember to keep wetting your hands and clay to prevent the clay from sticking to the hands, thus distorting it and pulling it out of centre. I have found that the most efficient way of doing this is to lift the water from the bowl with the cupped left hand and allow it to run down the fingers of the right hand which should be just touching the clay.

4  When the clay has been centred the next stage is called 'opening out'. This procedure, like centring, can be done in more than one way. The method I always use and teach is to lay the fingers of both hands on top of the clay with the long fingers meeting at a point in the centre of the lump. By applying pressure at the finger-tips with the long fingers forming the spear head, a well can slowly be sunk into the lump. This should terminate leaving enough clay left between fingers and wheel head to allow for cutting off and later turning. Pressure should again be applied at the finger-tips but this time against the walls of the form. This will cause the well to open out and should terminate when it is decided that the inside base diameter is big enough (Fig. 21). Use the side of the thumb to level off any imperfections on the base beginning at the centre and working outwards.

■ Fig. 21. Opening out.

5  The next stage is called 'thinning out'. Here the walls of the opened out clay are thinned into a basic cylinder shape from which the final form will be made. The thinning out is done by applying pressure to a point at the base of the inside right wall of the vessel with the left-hand finger-tips and at the opposite point on the outside right wall with the right-hand finger-tips or first-finger knuckle. As the wheel rotates this pressure will cause a

■ Fig. 22. Thinning out.

■ Fig. 23. Developing the shape.

ridge of clay to form above the fingers and knuckle. Now by lifting the fingers and knuckle vertically up the wall of the vessel with the same applied pressure, the clay will be forced to thin out and the cylinder will take shape and gain height (Fig. 22). Pressure should be reduced as the top of the cylinder is approached. The knuckling up should be done in one steady movement and not a series of jerky stages. The process is repeated until it is decided that the clay has been suitably thinned out and the cylinder is of the required height and diameter. The clay wall should be thicker at the base than at the rim.

Making a sound cylinder should be the first aim if one is going to make progress in throwing. Make a lot of small

ones, cutting some vertically down the centre with a wire to check the section of the wall.

These cylinders will be of no further use, but it is only by destroying some in this manner that any improvement can be measured.

6   When a good cylinder has been made the next stage is to create the intended form. This is done by thinning the clay further, working on the incoming clay at the right-hand side of the vessel. By applying pressure on the inside the form will fill out, and by applying pressure on the outside the form will close in (Fig. 23). Pressure from both hands circling the clay on the outside will narrow

the form. This is known as 'collaring' and is often used in shaping the neck of the vessel before the lip is given its final shape.

To make a pouring lip, place a wet finger and thumb against the neck of the vessel, about an inch or so apart (this of course being relative to the size of the vessel). Next, with a wet finger of the other hand, pull the vessel rim in between the fingers and thumb over and outwards (see Fig. 24). Care must be taken not to tear the clay and the neck of the vessel must be tall enough to allow for the pulling of a lip. A slight flare at the vessel rim will also make pulling the lip easier.

■ Fig. 24. Making a jug lip.

Forms with a wide middle and a narrow neck should be kept as narrow as possible at the rim from the time the cylinder is first thrown. If the neck is allowed to become too wide, severe collaring will only succeed in twisting it or narrowing it into a series of folds. Slight faults and unevenness at the neck and the lip may be trimmed off by gently pushing a corked needle through the clay towards a supporting finger on the inside of the form. Once cut through, the clay should come away in a tidy ring. If the fault is too severe the vessel should be scrapped and a fresh start made. Much time is wasted trying to prop, patch up or otherwise doctor faulty work which, if not a disaster in the making, will certainly fail in the firing. Forms which are too narrow for throwing with the hand on the inside of the vessel have to be worked using a wooden profile or sponge on a stick.

7    Finishing off the form is of course important. One must ensure that it is crisp and free from surface water, slip or any other untidy marks. First remove any water from inside the vessel, while it is rotating, with a natural sponge. If the neck of the vessel is very narrow, the sponge on a stick will have to be used or the vessel dried out before the neck is closed in. Water left in the vessel will either cause it to collapse due to excessive softening of the base, or crack as it dries out. Any messy slip on the outside surface can be removed by moving the natural sponge slowly up the spinning form and then by doing the same with the side of the right-hand little finger. A metal kidney scraper or rib tool (see Fig. 18(b)) may be used in the same way to remove stubborn slip or severe irregularities in the surface of the clay. Overdone, however, this treatment will result in the loss of the thrown quality.

The lip of the vessel may be given a very smooth finish by overlapping it with a wet piece of chamois leather, while the form is rotating. It is best to keep this leather with the sponge, in a bowl of water. Chamois leather which has been lost in the messy clay is usually only found again when the reclaimed clay is either wedged or even thrown.

Before the wheel is stopped, spare clay should be removed from the base of the vessel by slightly undercutting it with a pointed turning tool. This not only keeps things tidy but will also help to prevent unnecessary loss of clay when the vessel is cut from the wheel.

**8** The vessel is now ready for 'cutting off' and removing from the wheel. This is usually done with the wheel head stationary.

First wet the wheel head thoroughly by squeezing water on to it from a sponge. Then holding the wire taut, pass it from back to front beneath the vessel (Fig. 25). Repeat this once and then, applying finger-tip pressure at the front base of the vessel only, push it towards the back of the wheel using a slight twist action. Thumb pressure at the front base should then propel the vessel comfortably along the film of water on to the fingers spread in a tray arrangement at the edge of the wheel head (Fig. 26). Supported in this manner, the vessel can be transferred to a board for drying out to leather hardness.

■ Fig. 26. Removing the vessel from the wheel.

■ Fig. 25. Cutting off.

## Throwing bowls and dishes

While centring the clay is the same as for any other shape, the degree to which it is opened out and the direction in which the walls are thinned differ slightly. For example, it would be pointless to make a wide shallow bowl from a ball of clay opened out and thinned into a tall cylinder. The rim would tear long before it settled down into the bowl form. The procedure would be therefore to slightly open out the clay and then thin the walls from the centre of the lump diagonally outwards, rather than from base edge vertically upwards (see Fig. 27 overleaf). Too quick a shaping of the bowl, however, would probably result in it pancaking. To avoid this the thinning should be done so that the rim of the bowl is kept to its smallest possible diameter before the final shape is laid down. Leave enough clay at the base to support the wide rim and finish off the form with the wheel rotating very slowly.

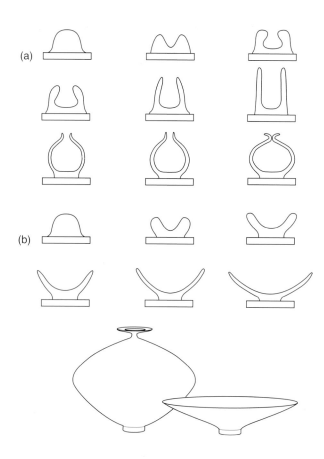

(a)

(b)

■ Fig. 27. Cross-section of the development of basic shapes. (a) The cylindrical shape; (b) The bowl shape.

Flat dishes are really an extension of the same technique with slight differences. Very wide flat forms are thrown from a much flatter lump or disc of clay which can be opened out with the heel of the hand rather than the fingers. This is done by pressing with the heel of the right hand into the centre of the clay leaving enough thickness at the base for cutting off and turning. Then with the fingers pivoting on the left hand, which is in the centring position, turn the heel out to the edge of the lump. This will open the clay out in almost one movement, leaving just a shallow wall and lip to throw. This technique will require some practice and the standard procedure for opening out will do just as well even if it takes a bit longer.

So far I have explained the procedure for throwing basic cylindrical and bowl shapes. Without wishing to be pessimistic, it is just as difficult to do as it is to explain on paper. Like other skills, a lot of practice and some good practical instruction is needed. At first things may not progress as smoothly as I have tried to explain them. The first difficulty will be centring the clay and keeping it there. It will want to go anywhere but in the centre of the wheel. This first stage must be mastered if any success is to follow. Opening out clay which is not centred will result in a vessel of uneven thickness, if one is made at all. It is also virtually impossible to re-centre a severely out-of-centre vessel. Do not be in too great a hurry. Master each stage before moving on to the next.

With very little development, a cylinder can have a handle attached for a mug, an outwardly dented rim plus a handle for a jug, and a fitting lid for a storage jar. Many bowl shapes may precede the perfect

■ Thrown stoneware.

cylinder as this is a much easier shape to throw. After all, opened out clay is not far removed from a thick-walled bowl and as the force of the wheel will throw the rim out if not checked, a bowl shape is easier to make than a cylindrical one.

## Points to remember in throwing

Here are a few points to remember which will ease the preliminary rough rides:

- Make sure that the clay is well prepared and plastic.
- Start with about half a dozen small balls of clay. If one fails there are still five to go at. Wrap them in polythene so that they remain in good condition.
- Drop the clay on to a damp wheel head, not a wet one. The clay should also be dampened, not wet, at this stage.
- Do not be tempted to maul the vessel while the wheel is stationary or crispness will be lost.
- Air pockets which persist, even after coning, come to the surface during the thinning of the walls. This air can be released by stopping the wheel and piercing the blobs with a corked needle or piece of wire. When throwing is resumed, the air will be squashed out. The point of corking the needle is that it will float if dropped into the water in the wheel trough.
- If any hard bits or foreign bodies are encountered in the clay during throwing, stop the wheel, carefully dig them out and fill up the hole with fresh clay.
- Work in a tidy manner. Keep the tools on the tool tray at the back of the wheel and check them at the end of each session. A corked needle misplaced in clay is potentially dangerous. Remember that, despite the popular myth about artists, an untidy workman is usually a bad one.

When confidence and skill have been developed in the elementary but very necessary stages of throwing, it is time to move on to more experimental forms and advanced throwing techniques. A slight change in curve anywhere on the form can completely alter its appearance. Varying the lips on vessels of similar basic form can make them look quite different. The variations of wide and narrow necks, short full forms and tall elegant ones are unlimited. Bowls, although seemingly limited in variation, can in the hands of a skilled thrower and artist vary from the elegant to the useful.

By varying lips and sides, sloping in or out, even flat dishes can be given their individuality. Then, of course, there is the wide range of domestic or utilitarian forms to consider where the fitting together of individual units into one whole is another challenge. Lids, spouts, handles and lugs are all made separately and then attached to the main shape. From this, one can progress to the making of sets or related forms such as mugs, jugs, storage jars, casseroles, soup- coffee- and tea-sets. Again let us consider each stage of throwing and the items to be made step by step.

## Pulled handles

The most satisfactory method of making handles for thrown shapes is to pull them out of a piece of clay which has been attached to the vessel. The procedure is as follows:

1. Take a small piece of prepared plastic clay from the same batch used for making the vessel. Roll the clay between dampened hands into a short roll shape thicker at one end than the other.
2. Grip the roll lightly between the first finger and thumb so that it is hanging vertically with the thick end protruding slightly above the finger.
3. Using the other hand, pat the thick end into the junction crevice of the finger and thumb. Rotate the roll in a half circle and repeat the action. This should make the thick end hammer-shaped, ideal for pushing on to the vessel to form the main joint. Squeeze the rest of the roll out into the rough handle shape with the fingers.
4. Select the attachment point on the vessel and using a pointed modelling tool roughen or tease the contact surface of both the vessel and the handle. I should point out here that the vessel will have been turned (a process to be explained later) and be of firm but damp consistency (leather hard).

**5**  Paint both teased surfaces with a light coat of slip made from the batch of clay (Fig. 28). The slip can be made by taking a small piece of clay from the batch and rolling it into a ball. Press the thumb into the centre to make a hollow. Fill the hollow with water and using a potter's brush, swill the water round until a quantity of slip forms.

**6**  Holding the vessel in one hand and the handle in the other, push the teased hammer head of the rough handle on to the corresponding point on the vessel (Fig. 29). Make the joint smooth with the finger and make it appear as though the added clay is an extension rather than an addition (Fig. 30).

**7**  Have plenty of water handy in a bowl. Hold the vessel horizontally so that the extended clay hangs down vertically. With the thumb and finger of the other hand forming an oval section, lightly grip the hanging clay at the joint and using sufficient water as a lubricant, gently but firmly pull down the length of the clay. This repeated action will thin out the clay until a suitable handle thickness has been achieved (Figs. 31 and 32 opposite). The section of the handle should be thicker at the joint thinning gradually towards the other end.

**8**  Decide where the length of clay is to be re-joined to the vessel and slightly roughen the surface at that point.

**9**  Brush a drop of slip on to this point and then, looping the clay to form the handle, re-join it on to the vessel (Fig. 33 opposite).

■ Fig. 29. Attachment.

■ Fig. 28. Applying slip to the teased surfaces.

■ Fig. 30. Smoothing out joint.

**10** Carefully return the vessel to the vertical position. Then make permanent the new joint by nipping off any excess clay and by smoothing the base of the handle on to the vessel with the first finger.

**11** Any unwanted marks at the handle joints or on the vessel can now be cleaned away with a damp natural sponge. The vessel is then allowed to dry slowly upside down so that the handle will settle into its natural curve.

Another method of pulling handles is to pull them out of a lump of clay and then attach them to the vessel. This method, while suitable for vessels too large to hold, involves too much mauling of the handle before it is attached to the vessel. The method I have explained, while perhaps more difficult for beginners, is well worth mastering for its directness and the fresh appearance of the finished handle.

■ Fig. 32. Pulling the handle.

■ Fig. 31. Pulling the handle.

■ Fig. 33. Lower attachment.

## Extruded handles

Forms which are thrown and then the whole of the outside turned to give a smooth, sharp and mechanical finish look out of place with a pulled handle on them. Hand finishes and machine finishes do not mix. A mechanical method is therefore used to make handles for this type of vessel.

Clay is forced through a hole in a metal plate, the shape of the hole being the handle section. The equipment required for extruding handles in this manner is called a 'dod' or 'wad box'. This is simply a metal cylinder with a screw ram at one end and the die plate at the other. Prepared clay is packed into the cylinder, then forced through the die plate with the

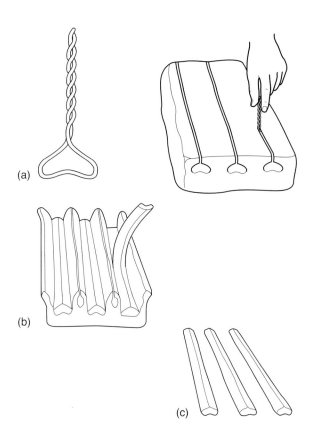

(a)

(b)

(c)

■ Fig. 35. Extruding a handle. (a) Pulling the wire through the clay; (b) Opening out the clay and removing extruded strips; (c) Lengths of extruded clay.

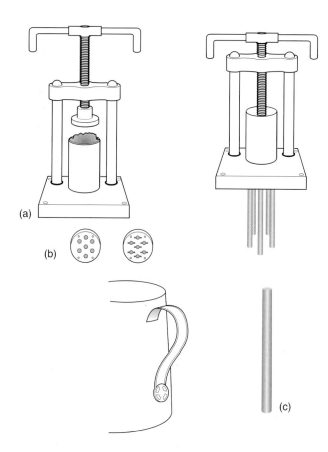

(a)

(b)

(c)

■ Fig. 34. Extruding the handle. (a) Dod or wad box; (b) Die plates; (c) Extruded strip cup and made into a handle.

screw ram (see Fig. 34). While equipment solely for this purpose is available, a pugmill with a die fitted over the end would make a perfect dod box. The extruded strip is then cut into lengths as required and the handles looped and attached to the vessel with slip. A variety of handles can be produced by interchanging different-shaped dies. While the dies may be purchased ready cut, schools may have facilities in the metal workshop for making them.

Handles may also be extruded by shaping a stiff wire into the handle section and then dragging it through a long block of prepared clay (see Fig. 35). The clay is then carefully opened out and the strip of cut clay removed. This method, while a cruder version of the first one, is a quick and simple way of demonstrating the extruding technique.

## Thrown handles

There are a variety of handles which may be thrown and are especially suited to the casserole type of form (see Fig. 36). Some are applied to the vessel as thrown, perhaps as one long one or two short ones either side (Fig. 36(a)). Others are made by cutting shallow, thrown rings in two across their diameter and by then applying the two halves to either side of the vessel (see Fig. 36(b)). These are known as lugs.

■ Thrown stoneware casseroles.

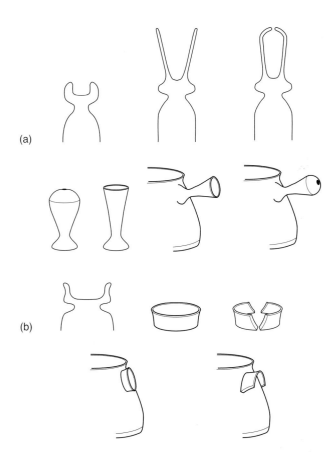

■ Fig. 36. Thrown handles. (a) Long handles; (b) Lug handles.

Thrown handles and lugs are fitted to the vessel when all are leather hard and after any turning has been done. All surfaces to be joined must be teased and painted with a light coat of slip made from the same clay. The additions are then pressed firmly into place, supporting the vessel on the inside with the hand. Finally all gaps and unwanted marks are filled in and smoothed out with modelling tool and sponge.

## Throwing lids

To continue with relating one unit to another, the making of lids is perhaps the next stage in developing the throwing technique. The making of lids can be divided into two groups – those which are thrown the right way up, as they would look on the vessel, and those which are thrown inverted. Lids thrown the right way up are basically shallow cylinders with enough clay left in the centre for the knob and the top of the cylinder folded outward to form a flange (see Fig. 37). This type of lid is turned on the underneath when leather hard. Lids thrown inverted are basically bowl shapes which are left either as a shallow bowl or further thrown with the flange on the side to hold the lid in place (see Fig. 38 opposite). A pillar of clay is left under the lid to be turned into a knob when leather hard.

The procedure for throwing lids the right way up is as follows:

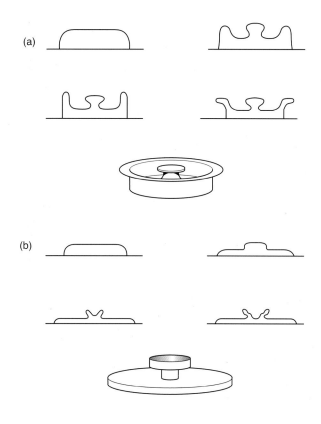

■ Fig. 37. Thrown lids. (a) Flange lid; (b) Flat lid.

1   Take a relative size piece of prepared clay, the same kind as for the vessel, and centre it to a flat rather than a cone shape. Use the side of the hand to flatten the top of the centred clay.

2   Leave a small amount of clay in the centre of the lump for the knob and open the clay out as for any small shallow cylinder.

3   Thin the walls into the vertical position and take a measurement with the callipers. This measurement should be slightly smaller than the inside diameter of the vessel rim. If the vessel has been made with a lid shelf or gallery below the rim, this measurement is, of course, the one to work to.

4   Work the solid clay in the centre of the cylinder into the intended knob form. Do this either by collaring the base with the finger-tips so that the solid grows and thins or by levelling off the top with the side of the finger, or by partially opening it out and levelling it off, etc. There are plenty of variations to practise and experiment with on the shape of the knob.

5   The final stage of shaping the lid is to bend the cylinder rim over, thus forming the flange. If the flange is going to rest on the rim of the vessel, the amount of cylinder turned over is mainly a decorative feature (Fig. 37(a)).

If the flange is going to rest on the gallery the amount of rim to bend over depends on the inside diameter of the vessel at the rim.

The diameter measurements of a lid should be slightly smaller than the corresponding measurements on the vessel. If, however, they are made the same size, the lid can be turned down when leather hard to give a good fit. Do not forget to make an allowance for any fitting areas which are to be glazed. A very good fit at the greenware stage might not fit at all with the additional thickness of glaze.

For throwing inverted lids the procedure is as follows:

1   Take an amount of prepared clay and centre it to a cone shape rather than a flat shape.

2   Collar with the second fingers just below the top of the centred clay. This will cause a mushroom shape to develop. The top of the mushroom will be used to throw the lid while the knob will be turned from the stalk at a later stage.

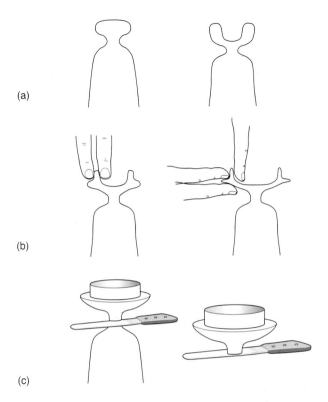

(a)

(b)

(c)

■ Fig. 38. Thrown lids. (a) Opening out the clay; (b) Making a flange; (c) Cutting off inverted lid.

**3** Open out the top of the mushroom as for any bowl shape but leave the walls unthinned (Fig. 38(a)).

**4** If the lid is to have a flange it is made at this stage by depressing the outer half of the unthinned wall with the first finger of the left hand while supporting the underneath of the bowl shape with the fingers of the right hand (Fig. 38 (b)). This action is terminated when the required depth of lid wall has been reached. The wall can now be thinned if necessary.

A gallery on the vessel for the lid flange to rest on is developed in a similar way with the flat finger-nail depressing the inside half of the rim to the depth required. Both gallery and flange can be trimmed with a turning tool when leather hard to give a good fit.

**5** The lid is then thrown outwards from the centre to the diameter required, measurements again being taken with the callipers to correspond with the vessel

measurements. The vessel measurements are, of course, taken as soon as it is made to ensure that there are no calculation errors due to shrinkage.

**6** For an inset lid the procedure is the same to step 3 and then the shallow bowl shape is thinned out to the required diameter and depth.

**7** Cutting off may be done with a wire taken through the supporting clay leaving enough to turn a knob. A quicker and more efficient way, however, is to cut into the base of the supporting column at a slight upward angle with a wet palette knife (Fig. 38(c)). This should be done while the wheel is revolving at a moderate speed. The lid will spin off on to the knife blade while the column is steadied with the fingers of the left hand.

These, then, are the basic types of thrown lid with the basic methods of how to make them. Whichever type of lid is made and whatever method is used to make it, the following points should be observed in its design:

■ The lid should be a reasonable fit and not slide about when the vessel is carried.

■ If the vessel is a coffee- or tea-pot, the lid should not fall out when the pot is tilted to pour, but be held in place by the gallery and lid wall.

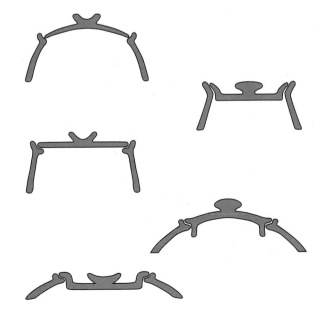

■ Fig. 39. Various lid fittings.

- A hole discreetly placed in the lid will help the pouring qualities of the pot.
- The lid, like any other addition to the vessel, should look an integral part of the whole unit, improving its appearance as well as fulfilling the function of a cover. (Some lid fittings are shown in Fig. 39 opposite.)

## Throwing spouts

While there is only one basic method of throwing a spout, variety can be given by changing the length, width and, of course, the shape of the vessel to which it is attached.

The method of throwing spouts is similar to that of making inverted lids and is as follows:

1 Centre the prepared clay and select the amount to be made into the spout by collaring as for the inverted lid. The amount of clay required can only be determined by trial and error and experience, for which there is no substitute.

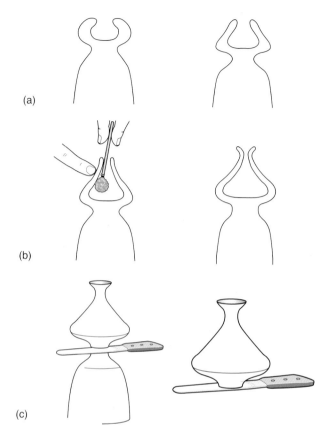

(a)

(b)

(c)

■ Fig. 40. Throwing a spout. (a) Opening out the clay: (b) Thinning the walls; (c) Cutting off the spout.

■ Earthenware tea set.

2 Open out the clay as for a lid but instead of thinning into a bowl shape, pull up into a cone-shaped cylinder keeping the diameter at the rim very narrow (Fig. 40(a)).

3 Once thinned, the cone is collared into dimensions of about 2½ in. diameter (6.08 cm) at the base, narrowing to ⅝ in. (1.5 cm) at the rim and about 3 in. (7.62 cm) high. The rim is usually given a flare which will eventually break the flow of the poured liquid and prevent dripping. Fingers are usually small enough to throw spouts. However, if a very narrow one is required, a soft thin brush or sponge on a stick can take the place of the finger for the inside throwing (Fig. 40(a)). Care must be taken not to press the brush too hard into the wall.

**4** The spout can be cut off with wire through the supporting clay, or preferably using the palette knife method (already explained) (Fig. 40(c)).

## Attaching the spout

The spout is attached after the vessel has been turned, before it is handled, and while vessel and spout are both leather hard. The procedure is as follows:

**1** Hold the spout at eye level behind and in contact with the vessel at the required height, angle and projection from the vessel (Fig. 41(a)).

**2** With a fettling knife, trace the outline of the side of the vessel on to the spout.

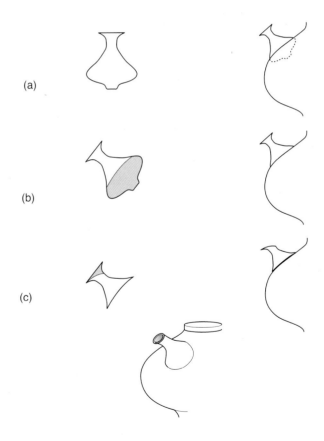

(a)

(b)

(c)

**3** Remove the spout from this position and cut around the tracing, thus removing unwanted clay from the spout (Fig. 41(b)).

**4** Place the spout in its intended position in the vessel and check that the angle and projection are right. Remove the spout to make any necessary adjustments, paring away clay from the base of the spout to secure a snug fit.

**5** Replace the spout to its intended position and mark round the base edge.

**6** Remove the spout again and, allowing for its thickness, mark a second line inside the first.

**7** If a tea-pot is being made, a number of small holes are drilled inside the smaller circle with a drill bit 1/8 in. (3.175 mm) or a mapping pen nib. This is to strain the tea leaves. If a coffee-pot is being made, a strainer of this sort is of little use for the sediment. A hole is therefore cut to the size of the inner line and the lack of a strainer offset by making the coffee-pot taller than the tea-pot. The coffee sediment will then settle at the bottom of this tall pot and never reach the level of the spout. However, in an age of instant coffee, this problem may never arise. The hole or holes should be cut at an angle to ensure the smooth flow of the liquid.

**8** Roughen up joining areas of spout and vessel and paint both areas with slip. Look down the barrel of the spout to check that there are no obstructions to impede the flow of the liquid.

**9** Holding the spout between finger and thumb, press it firmly into place on the vessel and weld in the joint to form a single unit (Fig. 41(c)). Light sponging should remove unwanted marks.

**10** The spout may be left with its round rim if this suits the overall design or it may be cut back at an angle to form the traditional type of pouring end (Fig. 41(c)). Care must be taken not to remove the bottom part of the flare or the drips will once again become a source of irritation.

Points to give special attention to when designing and making a spout are:

■ In the throwing process, take care the spout does not develop a twist. This is caused by too much throwing pressure and will unwind during the firing, turning the spout out of true and spoiling the

■ Fig. 41. Attaching a spout. (a) Marking the angle of attachment; (b) The spout cut for attachment; (c) Attachment showing cut back lip.

pot's appearance. Pouring is also impaired. If this tiresome fault becomes a habit, try to counteract the twist by attaching the spout out of true in the hope that it will twist into line when fired.

■ That the inside of the spout is clean enough, the neck is wide enough and the length is sufficient to make a good pourer.

■ That the spout is placed high enough on the vessel and at an angle so that the liquid does not flow out of the spout before the pot is full to the base of the lid.

■ That, like the lid and handle, it is an attractive and integral part of the overall form.

## Stack throwing

While this technique has more or less been described in throwing inverted lids and spouts, it is also very useful for throwing small shapes quickly. Bowls in particular can be produced in quick succession on top of the 'stack' without having to stop after each item is made to fix a new piece of clay to the wheel (Fig. 42).

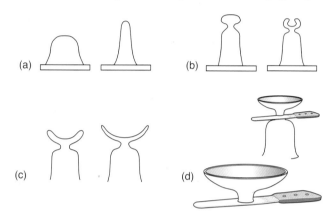

■ Fig. 42. Stack throwing for small bowls.

■ Modelled stoneware bull.

## Repeat throwing

Shapes repeated on the wheel never achieve the precise repetition of the cast or jigger and jolley shapes of industry. Nor should they if the character of wheel-made pottery is to be retained. However, this is neither a reason nor an excuse to avoid making wheel shapes of close similarity, and I am sure much satisfaction will be experienced when the skills necessary for this work have been mastered.

I would, therefore, suggest that repeat throwing be attempted in the following way:

1  Make a prototype of the items to be made, recording the weight of clay used, the diameter and the height. The diameter and height are measured with callipers and a gauge-post respectively. The gauge-post is usually a mobile item and is supplied as a wheel accessory to be positioned on the tool tray.
2  When the prototype is satisfactory, weigh out the number of pieces of clay needed for the set and wrap them in polythene until needed. Clay for handles should also be weighed out and then squeezed into the rough handle shape before wrapping in polythene.
3  Finally, make each piece to the measurements set on the callipers and gauge by one of the throwing techniques already explained.

## The use of bats

Large shapes, wide bowls and flat dishes are better thrown on bats attached to the wheelhead rather than on the wheelhead itself. When thrown, the shape can be removed with the bat thus avoiding possible distortion.

The most satisfactory bats are ¼ in. (6.350 mm) marine ply discs. These can be obtained in a variety of diameters and are attached to the wheelhead in one of two ways. The most common method is to flatten out plastic clay on to a damp wheelhead to a thickness of about half an inch and to then trim it level with a turning tool. The bat is then dampened, placed in the centre of the wheelhead and secured with several sharp blows from a blunt piece of wood.

The second method gives more security to the bat, but is more expensive. It really requires having a second wheelhead to which are fitted two small rivets, one in the centre and one near the edge (see Fig. 17, page 24). (An easy job for a school workshop.) Two corresponding holes are drilled through the bat which can be further secured to the wheelhead with a few small blobs of clay. These are flattened on the damp wheelhead before the damp bat is tapped on.

Whichever method is used the bat can easily be levered off with a stiff palette knife or spatula.

# Turning

When a thrown vessel has dried out to the leather hard stage it is ready for turning. This in simple terms means fixing the inverted vessel in the centre of the wheel and shaping or turning the underneath with a turning tool. Of course it is not quite as simple as that, although some schools of thought may argue that it is even simpler. In other words, the potter should not bother turning at all but leave the vessel as it was cut from the wheel with the twisted wire marks intact. Other contributions have been to cut the vessel from the wheel and to decorate the supporting clay with thumb or finger indentations. Examples of this treatment can be found in English pottery of the thirteenth and fourteenth century AD.

Pottery as an art form is, of course, always open to new ideas, but for me turning is an important follow-up to the throwing process, and has a considerable effect on the final form. Turning, with its variety of footrings, can make the thrown shape look light rather than heavy, elegant rather than clumsy. The footring, like the lip, can completely change the character of two similarly shaped vessels. The smooth crispness of the turned surface in contrast to the corrugated fluidity of the thrown surface, is often very pleasant and allows the potter to give a final individual stamp to the form of the pot, However, personal philosophies aside, the methods of turning are as follows.

■ Thrown and turned porcelain form.

with a wet sponge before it is placed over the dome. If, however, there is any doubt about the security of the bowl, three small pieces of plastic clay may be placed in a triangle arrangement around the rim of the vessel and pressed on to the rim and the dome. Also, before the bowl is set in place, estimate its thickness by feeling the shape between the finger and thumb, sliding them from the base to the rim.

2   Set the wheel in motion at a fairly fast speed. Select a sharp turning tool and with either a pointed end or corner, make a light cut into the base of the bowl at the estimated outer diameter of the footring.

3   The clay on the outside of the ring can now be turned away until the shape is satisfactory in appearance and thickness.

To do this, hold the cutting edge of the tool at a right angle to the clay on the right-hand side of the bowl and trim off the uneven base edge. Then slowly turn the clay away, moving inwards to the cut ring and downwards to a decided point on the wall of the vessel. The amount of clay turned away should be sufficient to give the form added beauty but obviously not so much that the vessel collapses or sags in the firing. Light tapping with the finger on the wall of the vessel will give some indication of

## Turning a bowl shape

1   Attach a firm lump of plastic clay to the wheelhead and turn it to fit the inside of the inverted bowl shape (see Fig. 43). The bowl should fit over this central dome like a cap in a position just above the wheelhead. This first procedure helps the easy centring of the inverted bowl, ensures that it is supported on the inside and prevents the rim from being damaged. The adhesion between the two damp surfaces should be enough to hold the vessel in place, particularly if the inside of the bowl is further dampened

■ Fig. 43. Placing the bowl on to the turned dome of clay.

thickness. The lighter the sound, the thinner the clay. This technique will only be developed with much practice and after many bottomless vessels. The safest way to assess thickness is to lift the vessel off the wheel and apply the finger and thumb test already described. The vessel can only be removed at this stage of turning, the reason being that it is very difficult to re-centre once the inside of the footring has been turned, but easy to turn the outside back to centre.

4   When the turning has been completed on the outside of the cut ring, the inside may be turned (Fig. 44). This section of the turning is better left to the last for two reasons. The first is the difficulty in re-centring the vessel as explained. The second is that by leaving this part unturned an estimate can be made of the thickness of clay turned from the outside of the ring.

Turning this section is done by starting in the centre of the inverted bowl and moving in a straight line to the edge, working from the centre to the right.

Turn the whole base level and after deciding on the thickness of the footring, make a second incision. Begin turning the clay out from the centre to this ring which, of course, will form the inner edge of the footring.

The depth of footring and the amount of clay cut away will depend on the thickness of clay left after throwing, the type of footring required and consideration for the overall shape.

■ Stoneware form.

## Turning a tall or bulbous shape

Shapes from the bowl to the cylinder can be turned in the way described. Cylindrical mug shapes can therefore be supported on the inside by a small disc of clay rather than a dome, with three pieces of clay on the outside for extra support. However, when the neck of the vessel is narrow or the belly of the vessel is wider than the neck, a hollow form or chuck has to be turned out of a lump of relatively firm clay and the vessel set inside this to a suitable depth for support (see Figs. 45 and 46 overleaf).

The procedure for turning is as before, although the type of footring will vary (see Fig. 47 overleaf). If for any reason the surface of the vessel has to be turned below the support line after the base turning is finished, the chuck can be hollowed out further to accommodate the vessel the right way up. In this way the whole of the outside form can be turned. I would suggest that some of the pot's appeal will be lost if all evidence of the thrown surface is removed.

■ Fig. 44. Turning the inside of the footring.

**pottery**

■ Fig. 45. Placing the jug shape into the turned chuck.

■ Fig. 46. Securing the vessel with three pieces of clay.

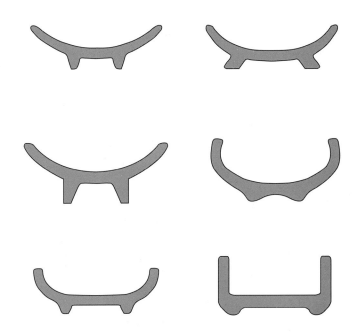

■ Fig. 47. A selection of turned footings.

## Turning lids and saucers

Basically the methods of turning have been explained, but as experience and individuality progress, modifications may be made to these to cope with original design, etc. For example, I turn flange and inset lids using a variation of the hollow chuck technique. To make the well in a saucer, I stick the saucer, right way up, to the flattened dome of clay used in turning the outside. A light wetting of both contact surfaces is enough to hold the saucer in place for this small job. Some may prefer to throw the well in the saucer, but I find it easier to obtain a successful fit between cup and saucer if the well is made at this stage. A sponge will remove any unwanted sharp edges and callipers will check the measurements.

## Tools used for turning

A selection of turning tools is shown in Fig. 48. These may be purchased from the potter's merchant, but can be made from 1 in. (25.40 mm) hoop iron.

The end inch is bent over at right angles, filed to shape and sharpened. Other tools can be made from hardened spring steel by bending them to shape and binding them to wooden handles.

Turning tools must be regularly sharpened and held at the correct angle when turning, otherwise chattering will occur on the surface of the vessel which is both unattractive and bad craftsmanship.

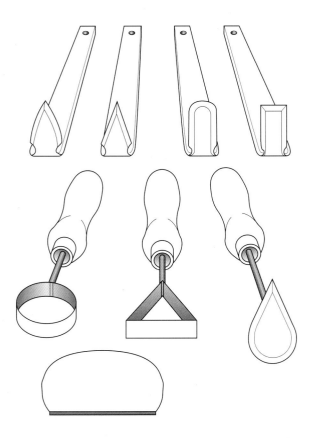

■ Fig. 48. A selection of turning tools.

■ Porcelain bowl.

# Slab shapes

This is the hand method of making angular pots which are a contrast to the round and oval forms of pinching, coiling and throwing. The method lends itself to constructional and sculptural pottery rather than to utilitarian ware, although members of my evening class get endless satisfaction in producing hundreds of butter dishes and plant containers in this way.

■ A variety of slabbed shapes.

While slab forms tend to be variations on a four-sided theme, there are no hard and fast rules about this. The only limitations are that the form must serve its intended purpose and that the sides must obviously hold together in firing.

The method for making a four-sided slab shape with base is as follows:

1 Prepare a quantity of plastic clay to a firmer consistency than for coiling or pinch ware.
2 Take a proportion of this clay and block it on the bench top.
3 Flatten the block with the heel of the hand to a thickness of approximately ½ in. (12.70 mm).
4 Roll the flattened clay level with a rolling-pin to a thickness of no less than ¼ in. (6.350 mm) (Fig. 53 [page 49]). These thicknesses are, of course, relative to the size of shape being made. Bigger shapes need thicker sections.

   Roll the clay in a forward and diagonal manner to give even pressure over the whole mass. Keep lifting and moving the clay to a drier area of the table so that it spreads out as it is rolled and does not stick to the working surface. Alternatively, the clay can be rolled out on a square of hessian or cloth which will prevent it from sticking. Also sprinkling fine sand on the table will help the clay to roll out very easily and prevent sticking. It will give a texture which, if unwanted, can be turned to the inside of the vessel. The disadvantage of sand is that, if the clay is of smooth texture, surplus clay cannot be returned to the smooth clay bin.

   A uniform flatness can also be achieved by rolling the clay out between two parallel strips of wood of the correct thickness, with the rolling-pin spanning them. This method will limit the size of clay to be rolled out to the length of the rolling-pin. Mastering the diagonal and forward technique is more spontaneous and without this limitation.
5 When the clay is ready, mark and cut out the largest rectangle possible on its surface using a ruler, straight edge and palette knife. An old knife with a thin blade or broken hacksaw blade will do. This will trim off untidy edges and leave an even slab of clay to subdivide into the slabs for the vessel. These slabs may be divided in one of

■ Fig. 49. Cutting out the slabs with the aid of a templet.

the following ways: either by measuring out the necessary number of slabs, cutting out the first one and then using it as a templet for the rest or by cutting out a templet in paper or card first and cutting around this (Fig. 49). At this stage keep any spare strips of rolled-out clay as they may come in useful later.

6   If the vessel is to have an impressed decoration (see chapter 4) it is perhaps better done at this stage while the clay is firmly supported on the bench (Fig. 50). When the slabs are assembled support could be given using a flat piece of wood held inside the vessel.

7   Before assembly, joining areas of the slabs should be teased and given a light coating of slip made from the same clay.

8   The slabs can then be joined as shown in Fig. 51 placing one teased surface firmly on to another and smoothing the clay together on both the inside and outside of the joint. A modelling tool or long painting brush handle will get to any awkward inside joints. The slab vessel should now look like a box with open ends.

9   Lift the box shape upright. The joints must be sound or they will spring open during the drying out, or more annoyingly, during the firing. At this stage it is worth giving the joints an extra nip with the finger and thumb. Any unwanted marks can be smoothed out later with a kidney scraper.

■ Fig. 50. Applying an impressed or stamped decoration.

■ Fig. 51. Assembling the slabs.

10  The four sides are now ready for a base. Place the box on to a spare piece of rolled-out clay. Allow for a small amount of extra clay around the edge of the walls and cut the base out.

11  Lift the box off the base and prepare areas to be joined. Press the walls firmly on to the base and smooth the extra clay on to the walls to make a strong joint (Fig. 52).

12  Any untidy edges can now be cleaned up with a metal scraper and sponge, care being taken not to remove too much clay at the joints and so weaken them.

■ Fig. 52. Fitting the base.

This, then, is the basic method of slab work and provides the ground from which experimental work can develop.

Bending and folding slabs of clay is at least worth a thought. For example, a slab of clay wrapped loosely around a rolling-pin which has first been wrapped in newspaper and joined at the overlap will make a cylinder shape very quickly. A combination of the slab method with other forms of hand building could also prove interesting and successful.

# Moulded shapes

The use of moulds in which to fashion clay dates back to pre-wheel times but the potential of moulded pottery was not fully realized until the discovery of plaster of Paris. While industrial pottery is now almost entirely made with the aid of plaster moulds, mainly for mass-production reasons, moulded pottery can only satisfy a certain amount of the artist potter's needs. These are generally the making of useful backgrounds for creative decoration.

As moulding is mainly an industrial method of pottery-making, there are books which deal with the subject more fully than I intend to do here. I will outline the principles of moulded shapes to a point where in my opinion studio pottery ends and industrial pottery begins.

Shapes made with the aid of moulds can be dealt with in two sections. These are pressing and casting.

## Pressing

This is a method generally used for making shallow dish forms in which the clay is fashioned by forcing it to follow the contours of a plaster mould. There are two kinds of pressmould. One is the convex type where clay is pressed over the mould and the other is the concave type where clay is forced into the mould. While many favour the convex type, I generally use concave moulds and would always recommend the beginner to use this type for the following reasons:

- The shape of the dish can be seen without having to imagine its reverse form.
- It is often worth leaving the dish in the mould for support when using incised, sgraffito or other methods of decoration which require pressure on the surface of the clay.

Whichever type is preferred, the making of both kinds of mould will be explained in the section on mould-making. The procedure is as follows:

1   Flatten the prepared clay with the heel of the hand into the rough outline shape of the dish. Roll this clay out level as explained in the making of a slab pot (Fig. 53). Clay can also be rolled out on a cloth such as hessian for press-moulding. The advantage of using this method is that the hessian supports the clay when it is being lifted on to the mould, thus preventing it from tearing.

2   When the clay has been rolled out, trim around the edge with a palette knife. This will tidy the slab up and is a check for any unevenness of section.

3   Make sure that the mould is clean and free from old dry slip. Lift the clay from the bench so that it hangs down like a cloth and carefully drape it across the mould (Fig. 54). Bigger pieces of clay, if not on hessian, can be transferred to the mould by supporting them on the rolling-pin. If the clay is draped across the mould with the smooth rolled outside face down to the mould, any cracks on the underneath of the clay will be visible and can be smoothed or filled when the dish is shaped.

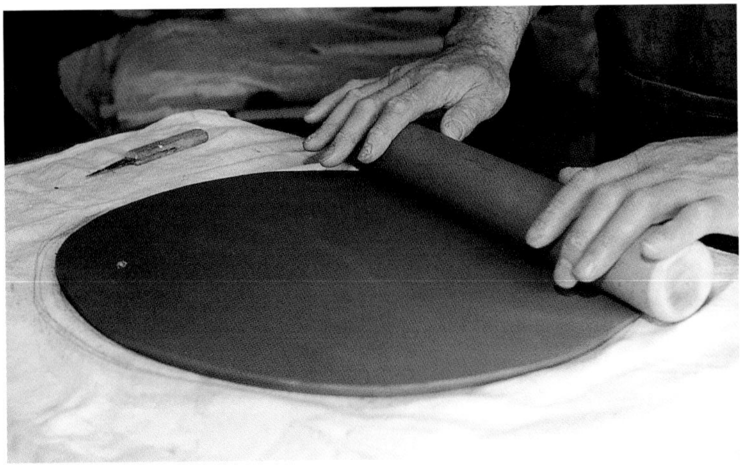

■ Fig. 53. Rolling the clay level.

■ Fig. 54. Placing the clay into the mould.

**4**  Carefully feed the clay into the mould from the edges pressing it very gently to the sides and base with the fingers. This must be done very carefully otherwise the fingers will press into the clay and the hollows may be difficult to remove.

**5**  When the clay is sitting firmly in the mould, smooth around the form with a damp sponge. Surplus clay may now be trimmed from the edge of the dish with the wire (harp or bass wire) held taut between the finger and thumb of both hands, or alternatively a bow cutter. Whichever is used, the wire should be kept as close to the mould as possible (Fig. 55).

**6**  The surface of the dish can now be finished by smoothing the clay with the curved side of a wet rubber kidney (Fig. 56). Smoothing with the flat side of the kidney around the edge of the dish will give this a finish. There should be no water left in the dish when the smoothing out is finished as this will tend to repel slip used for decoration and may cause cracking.

■ Fig. 55. Trimming off surplus clay.

The dish is now ready for impressed, incised or relief decoration, slip application or underglaze painting (when dry), all of which will be explained later on. If no pre-firing decoration is required the dish may be turned out of the mould when leather hard and the underneath and edges sponged clean. It can then be set aside to dry out in readiness for biscuit firing. To turn the dish out of the mould, place a board over the mould and dish and turn everything over. A light tap on the mould base should release the dish.

Making a dish on a convex mould is as explained for a concave one, the only real difference being that the clay is pressed over the mould rather than into it.

Shapes made with the aid of a simple dish mould do not have to become thousands of unwanted ash trays. There is plenty of scope for constructional work by joining dish shapes together (as for slabware), and with imaginative cutting they can be used in conjunction with coiling, etc. Much can be done with coiled lips and footrings.

■ Fig. 56. Finishing off the surface of the dish.

## Casting

This is the method where casting slip (differing from decorating slip due to its dispersal with deflocculant (see Glossary) rather than water) is poured into a plaster mould. The plaster, being porous, absorbs moisture from the slip and a layer of clay of even thickness forms around the inside of the mould. As soon as this layer is thick enough (after approximately 15 minutes' casting) the excess slip is poured out of the mould. The cast and mould are then left upside down, spanning two pieces of wood, to drain and dry. As soon as the cast is leather hard, it can be removed from the mould and handles etc. attached. The shape can then be cleaned up if necessary and set aside to dry out.

There are some points to remember when casting. These are as follows:

- Remember to stir the slip thoroughly before use, and keep it in an airtight container when not required immediately.
- If the slip has been standing unused for a number of weeks, pass it through an 80-mesh sieve before using.
- Make sure the mould is clean and free from old slip which will spoil the cast. Make sure also that the mould is level to prevent uneven casts. A spirit-level will make this check very quickly.
- Pour the slip slowly down the side of the mould at first so that air is not trapped in the bottom. The process can be speeded up when the base is covered. The mould is then filled to just above the rim allowing for a fall in the level of slip as moisture is absorbed.
- The usual time for casting is between 10 and 30 minutes, depending on the properties of the casting slip and the dryness of the mould. The level of the slip may have to be topped up during this time.

Cast sheep.

- Pour the excess slip out with the mould held at an angle to avoid a blob forming at the bottom of the cast.
- Handles are cast in a two-piece mould and attached to the vessel with a blob of casting slip.
- Moulds have a limited life mainly due to the corrosive effect of the deflocculants so do not expect them to go on for ever.

# Simple mould-making

While mould-making is often a chore, and moulds may be purchased from the supplier, the method of making them is not too difficult and individuality requires this discipline. Making a mould involves taking an impression in plaster of Paris of the model shape which has first been made in solid plastic clay or plaster. While the number of pieces in a mould depends on the design of the model, the principles of mould-making are much the same no matter what number are used. Therefore, moulds of one or two pieces should be sufficient for the studio potter's needs.

### Making a one-piece pressmould–non circular

1   Make working drawings of the intended shape to show the side and end elevations and plan.
2   Cut concave profiles in stiff card of the end and side elevations. A profile of the plan can be outlined on the modelling board.
3   Build up plastic clay inside the plan outline to the estimated proportions of the inverted shape.
4   Allow this clay to become firm and then carefully pare away the surplus clay with a metal kidney scraper and profile tool until the model is produced. Check the progress of the work continually with the cut profiles and the plan on the card (Fig. 57(a)).
5   Smooth out the surface of the model with a wet sponge and rubber kidney palette, making sure that the edge is very neat. The finish must be glass smooth as any irregularities will cast into the plaster and register on subsequent ware.
6   Place boards around the shape allowing approximately 1½ in. (38.10 mm) border. Mix and pour in the plaster as explained on page 18. To ensure that the plaster is the same thickness in the base of the mould as the sides, mark a point on the shuttering 1½ in. (38.10 mm) above the base of the model. The plaster should then be allowed to fill up to this level. Remember to seal all the board joints with clay on the outside before the plaster is

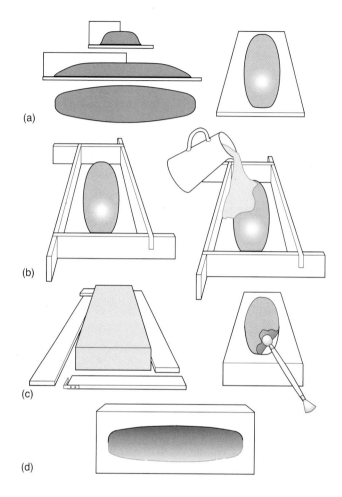

(a)

(b)

(c)

(d)

■ Fig. 57. Making a one-piece pressmould – non-circular. (a) End elevation, side elevation, plan, templates and finished model; (b) Assembling boards and pouring plaster; (c) Removing shuttering and clay model; (d) Finished concave mould.

poured. Tap the modelling board after pouring to remove air bubbles and to level off the plaster (Fig. 57(b)).
7   When the plaster has set, remove the shuttering and then remove the clay model. This is usually done with a modelling tool, taking a small piece of clay out at a time. (Fig. 57(c)). If the clay has shrunk sufficiently or the mould is very shallow, the model may lift out in one piece. In whatever way it is removed, great care must be taken not to damage the mould.

**8**  Finally, bevel the edges with a plaster or surform plane to prevent chipping and put the mould in a warm place to dry out.

If a convex (hump) mould is required, a positive can be made from the negative in the following way. Wipe the negative mould clean and paint the surface with a solution of soft soap and water, or potter's size. Apply about three coats at five-minute intervals, wiping off excess lather with a damp sponge. This is called 'sizing' and will render the treated plaster temporarily non-adhesive to the new plaster when the positive impression is taken. Fill up the mould with plaster and before it has set, a tube of stiff card should be placed on the plaster. The edge of the card should be 1½ in. (3.81 cm) from the edge of the plaster and 5 in. (12.70 cm) high. This should also be filled with plaster to form the foot of the mould. When everything has set hard, the positive should easily come away from the negative. If required, subsequent negative moulds can be made from the positive in a similar way.

## Making a one-piece pressmould–circular

Unless the shape is very large, circular models can be turned in leather hard clay on a bat on the wheel, and the surface finished off as before. An alternative to the board shuttering is linoleum or cottle sheeting bent around the model and secured with string or a strong elastic band. This will give the outside of the mould a circular rather than square shape.

## Making a one-piece drop-out mould for casting

As its name implies, this type of mould for cast pottery is made in one piece and, when the clay shape has been cast, the design of the mould allows the shrinking shape to drop out.

The mould can be a shallow dish pressmould, having a dual purpose or a deep cylindrical beaker mould made by turning the model on a wheel as explained. The point is that for a drop-out mould the line of the shape must widen from the base to the rim without any irregularities in between, thus preventing the cast

from dropping out when contraction takes place (Fig. 58).

## Making a two-piece mould for casting

After the principle of making a split mould is understood, the making of moulds of more than two pieces is mainly a matter of thought and time. Much can be achieved with a two-piece mould without crossing the border into mass-production.

One-piece moulds are all right for shapes that open out from base to rim, but any design which has even the slightest bulge inwards or outwards between these

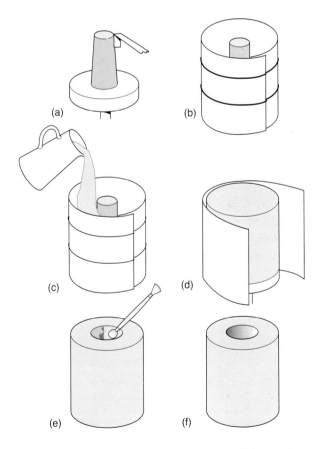

■ Fig. 58. Making a one-piece drop-out mould for casting. (a) Turning the model; (b) The cottle sheeting in place; (c) Pouring the plaster; (d) Removing the cottle; (e) Removing the model; (f) The finished mould.

**pottery**

points will require a mould of a least two pieces. The two-piece mould can, therefore, cope with any shape which will allow the mould to be pulled away in two halves without being locked by any little piece of the shape protruding in the wrong direction. Thought and careful design will eliminate this possibility. A simple two-piece mould would be made in the following way:

1  Make the model shape by one of the methods explained, i.e. turned on a wheel, hand fashioned, etc. Decide in which direction the mould is going to pull apart and check that there is nothing in the line of the form which will prevent this.

2  Set the model half-way into a block of firm clay leaving the same border at the base of the model as at the sides (see Fig. 59). This will be the break-point of the mould and must be worked out accurately, otherwise the mould will not open cleanly or the cast may be trapped in one half of the mould. The top of the model can fit flush to the edge of the clay block. The spare (see Glossary) which forms the shape of the rim on many moulds and also allows for trimming is unnecessary on a simple two-piece mould. However, the use of a spare is illustrated in Fig. 59.

3  Make three notches or hollows in the smooth top of the block of clay (see Fig. 60). The hollows will cast as domes on the first half of the mould, and hollows in the second half. These will act as keys so that one half of the mould is always located in exactly the right place with the other half. I make my hollows by twisting a small coin one revolution into the clay.

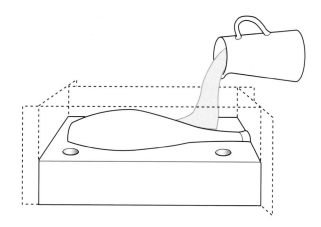

■ Fig. 60. Casting the first half of the mould.

4  Put the four boards around the block of clay as already explained, not forgetting to make the plaster level mark on the inside. No sizing is necessary if the model and support are made of clay. Fill the plaster up to the mark.

5  When the first half of the mould has set, carefully remove the boards. Turn the plaster and clay block over so that the half mould is underneath. Very carefully remove the clay block. This should leave the model sitting in the first half of the mould ready for the second half to be cast.

6  Size the plaster with soft soap, put up the boards and cast the second half of the mould up to the mark previously made.

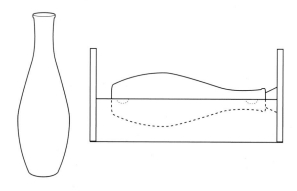

■ Fig. 59. Making a two-piece mould for casting. Model and spare set in block of clay.

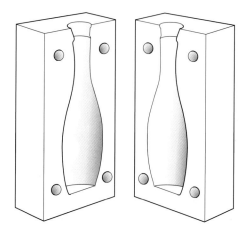

■ Fig. 61. Finished mould.

7  When the plaster has set, remove the boards and pull the two halves apart. Remove the model carefully which, if in good condition, can be used for making more moulds. If the model is damaged, a plaster one can be cast from the mould just made, but do not forget to size the plaster surfaces thoroughly.

8  Lightly bevel the edges of the mould to prevent chipping and put in a warm place to dry out. When casting, the two halves can be held together with strong elastic bands.

The making of a two-piece handle mould is illustrated in Fig. 62.

If a concave rather than a flat base is required on the finished shape, this would mean making a third piece to the mould and is an easy job. The mould is made in the same way as the two-piece mould except that at

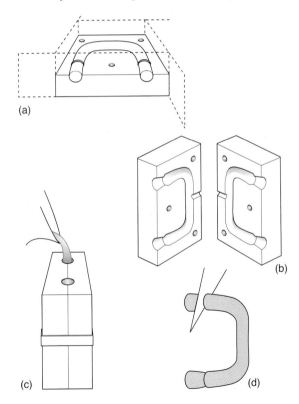

■ Fig. 62. Making a two-piece handle mould for casting or pressing. (a) Making the mould; (b) The finished mould showing spares and air escape hole; (c) Pouring casting slip into assembled mould; (d) Trimming spares from cast handle.

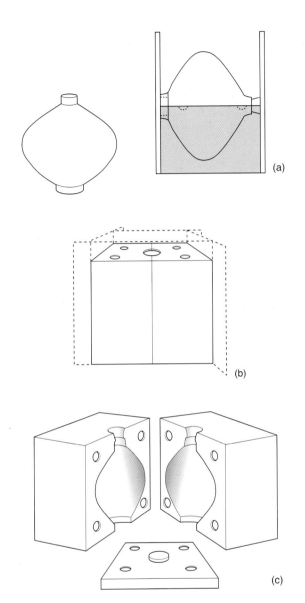

■ Fig. 63. Making a three-piece mould for casting. (a) Model set in block of clay; (b) Two pieces of the mould in position ready for casting the third piece; (c) Finished mould.

(62(b)), no border is allowed at the base of the model and the boarding is placed flush to it top and bottom (see Fig. 63(a)). When both halves have been cast, they are kept together with the model inside and turned bottom up. Boards are placed around again, the plaster sized and the third piece cast (see Figs 63(b) and (c)).

■ Tile with slip inlaid decoration.

# Tiles

Tiles were used as early as 3500 BC by the Egyptians. They were made from a clay and sand composition and covered with a turquoise glaze. While tiles were originally used to cover and decorate floors, walls and ceilings, they are now found on cheese-boards, table-tops, etc. and as an alternative to paintings and fabrics as framed wall decorations.

Tiles produced by the industry are generally of the 4¼ in. × 4¼ in. or 6 in. × 6 in.(108 mm × 108 mm or 152 mm × 152 mm) type and ⅛ in. thick. The dimensions of a tile need only be governed by the method in which they are made, the size of the kiln in which they are fired and, of course, the job for which they are intended. Therefore a tile may be as small as a piece of mosaic or as big as a panel of clay 2 in. (5 cm) thick. Pieces of mosaic are usually put together to make bigger areas of decoration after firing. The big

clay panel would be cut into smaller sections along suitable lines in the design and then reassembled after firing. Gouging clay out of the back of these large tiles while leaving the edge intact will lighten them and help them dry out.

The uses to which tiles may be put, and the sort of tiles to make, are dependent on the ingenuity and skill of the artist. Tiles are particularly useful in a teaching situation for illustrating different methods of surface decoration. Children also enjoy making small cut-out tiles, as little skill is required, and the finished article can look extremely attractive.

Tiles can be made in a number of ways. The usual ones are cutting from a slab of rolled-out clay, cutting from a block of plastic clay, pressing in a mould or pressing in a tile press.

## Tiles made from a slab of clay

The method of rolling out an even slab of clay has already been described and is the same for tiles as for slabs or pressed shapes. The rolled-out clay is allowed to dry slightly until it is just softer than leather hard. It can then be cut up into tiles using a card templet, a straight edge and a thin knife. Alternatively, tile cutters can be used (see Fig. 64(c)).

Assuming the tile is of even thickness, the secret of keeping it flat is in the drying out and firing. Tiles should be allowed to dry out very slowly and evenly on both sides. If one side dries quicker than the other it will obviously shrink more and the tile will curl up. This can happen to a lesser extent in the firing. The tile needs to be dried and fired with air freely circulating around it. Tiles will dry out in this manner if placed in saddles. The firing of them will be dealt with in Chapter 6. For convenience, I often dry out tiles on the textured side of flat pieces of hardboard. The air can get to the tiles because of the textured surface and by turning them over occasionally they remain reasonably flat.

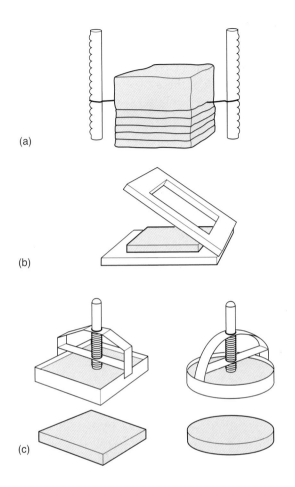

**4** Repeat this process moving the wire one notch up for each cut. The block can then be separated into tiles.

This method might also be tried for slab shapes and pressed dishes.

## Tiles pressed from a mould

Firm plastic clay can be pressed from the block into a plaster or wooden mould. Once the clay has been pressed into the mould it can be levelled off with a straight edge. The one illustrated in Fig. 64 (b) is made from 1½ in. × ½ in. (38 mm × 12 mm) beechwood and hinged to a base board. The inside of the frame should be slightly bevelled so that after the tile has been made, the frame can be lifted and the tile pushed gently out.

Test tiles can be made using one of the methods described, and fired before the tile frame is constructed. Measuring a test tile before and after firing will show the exact shrinkage. The tile frame can then be made to allow for this. If different clays are used for the tests, an average shrinking rate could be used for calculating the frame size.

Generally speaking the shrinkage will be about one-eighth, but testing is the only way of reducing the hit and miss element.

## Tiles made in a tile press

This is the industrial method of producing very thin tiles with little shrinkage and warpage. Semi-dry powdered clay is put into the die of the tile press and subjected to severe pressure. The tile is released by a foot- and hand-operated lift mechanism. Presses and dies can be purchased in different sizes and all the specifications are given in the suppliers' catalogue (see list of suppliers).

This is obviously the best method for anyone wishing to mass-produce standard thin tiles on which to apply painted or printed decoration. However, it does not offer the same scope for surface decoration as the other three methods.

■ Fig. 64. Making tiles. (a) Cutting tiles from a block of clay; (b) Pressing tiles in a wooden mould; (c) Cutting tiles out of a slab using tile cutters.

## Tiles made from a block of plastic clay

This is a very easy method of tile-making and is as follows:

**1** Block a piece of plastic clay and allow it to become firm.
**2** Take two pieces of dowelling of equal length and cut corresponding notches along their length, these being the thickness of the tiles.
**3** Loop a length of harp wire at both ends and link it on the bottom notches of the dowelling. Pull the wire tight and, keeping the dowel ends on the bench, pull through the block of clay (see Fig. 64(a)).

# 4

# Decoration before firing

$\mathsf{F}$ ew potters can resist the temptation to apply decoration to at least some of their work even though the form of a pot may be complete in itself. Tiles and flat shapes lend themselves to surface decoration while three-dimensional shapes perhaps need more consideration.

■ Porcelain forms with inlaid decoration.

The decoration may be as simple as a surface texture or an interesting glaze. It may be as complex as some of the sgraffito and incised ware to be found throughout pottery history. But whatever the design of the decoration, it has surely only one purpose and that is to improve the pot's appearance. Therefore, careful consideration must be given to this if the reverse is to be avoided. Not only must the decoration enhance the form but the method in which it is applied must also be suitable for the type of ware being made. For example, slip applied with a brush may look lively on one pot and clumsy on another.

The following methods of decoration have all been extensively used at some period of pottery history. Their freshness and appeal would therefore seem to depend on the originality of the design and the type of ware on which they are used. It is with this thought in mind that they are listed and explained.

# Incising

This is a method of decoration in which the design is engraved or incised into the leather hard ware using some sort of pointed tool. The end of the tool can have a narrow or broad point depending on the lines of the design. However, the cutting edges of the tool must be sharp to give a clean cut into the clay.

Good incising tools can be made from bamboo or cane. The cane can be sawn up into 6 in. (15.24 cm) lengths and the ends sharpened to a variety of widths.

Many fine examples of incising are to be found on the celadon-glazed porcelain pots of the Chinese Sung period.

# Impressing

This must be one of the earliest methods of applying decoration to a clay surface. It is done simply by pressing some firm object into the soft surface of the clay.

The decoration may be just a texture as a result of beating with rough grained wood. It is usually, however, a more contrived design applied with a stamp in some sort of repeated order (Fig. 50 [page 47]).

Impress stamps can be made in the following ways:

- Carve the design directly onto wood or plaster.
- Carve the design into clay and biscuit fire.
- Carve the design into clay and cast in plaster.

A roller stamp can be made in clay and biscuit fired, or carved in wood. The roller is then attached to a wire handle.

It is also worth experimenting with miscellaneous objects as stamps. These could include a ruler end, a screw head or the end of a plastic tube.

# Relief

A development of direct impressing is to stamp the design on to thin pads of clay, and to apply these to the leather hard ware with slip. The pads of clay can also be attached to the ware and then stamped.

Another type of relief decoration is produced by first pressing the clay relief in a negative mould. The relief is then removed from the mould and applied to the ware. This method is generally known as 'sprigging'. While sprigged decoration can be found elsewhere on pottery, none is technically better than that on Wedgwood's jasper stoneware. Here the sprigged decoration is white and set against a coloured background.

While the theory of sprigging is easy to understand, there is quite a bit more to the method, which is as follows:

1   Make the mould. This can be done either by taking a negative plaster impression of a positive clay model, or by biscuit firing the model and taking an impression in a clay block, which is then fired. Whichever method is used the moulds should be small, approximately 2 in. × 3 in. (5.08 cm × 7.62 cm). The relief should not contain undercuts which will prevent its release from the mould.

**2** Press plastic clay into the mould with the thumb and level off with a metal palette knife or scraper.

**3** Remove the relief by pressing lightly down on it with the flat of the knife and then lifting. The relief should come away sticking to the knife. If the relief refuses to come from the mould in one go, it can usually be persuaded by repeating the action. Begin at one end of the relief and work slowly to the other. Some biscuit moulds, however, are so porous that just turning them over and tapping is enough to release the relief.

**4** Once released, the relief can either be placed flat side down on a damp surface until more pressings are taken, or it can be transferred on the wet palette knife directly into position on the ware. The work should be leather hard and the area of contact dampened with a sponge. Slip can be used but on the industrial production line the damp surfaces and light finger pressure seem to be enough to adhere the relief perfectly. The less fuss in attachment, the more crisp the finish.

**5** The whole decoration is then assembled from a variety of small reliefs by fitting them one to another.

Relief decoration can also be built up by working directly on the surface of the ware with plastic clay. I feel that this method requires experimentation rather than explanation.

# Inlaying

This method of decoration is really one stage on from incising and impressing. It involves running or dabbing thick slip, of a contrasting colour, into the incised or impressed decoration on the ware. The slip should be applied to damp, firm ware and be filled to a level higher than the surface of the ware. When both clays are leather hard the surface can be shaved level with a metal scraper. This will give a sharp definition to the design.

The tradition of inlaid pottery has been to use red clay inlaid with white or vice versa. Medieval tiles decorated in this way can still be seen in some of our

■ Earthenware plate with slip decoration.

churches. However many more contrasting colours are now possible with the wide range of clay stains available. It would therefore appear that inlaying offers much scope for development.

# Marbling

This is the technique of intermingling different coloured slips on a clay surface to give a marbled effect. While this type of decoration was popular on English slipware of the seventeenth and eighteenth centuries, the resulting effect is mainly due to chance rather than design. It is, however, a good method for catching the interest of the beginner because only a small amount of skill is required to give a decoration with some standard of finish.

Marbling can be done on tall ware but is more suited to flat ware. It is carried out in the following way:

1  If the decoration is to be applied to a tile, the background slip should be poured from a jug while the damp tile is held at an angle of 45 degrees. Begin pouring at one of the top corners of the tile, moving the jug slowly along the top edge to the other corner and allow a steady flow of slip to cover the tile face.

■ Fig. 66. The finished marble effect.

For a bowl or a pressmould dish the slip can be poured into the hollow of the ware, rolled around the surface once and then the excess poured out (Fig. 65). As with most slip applications, the ware should be damp but firm. The application of large areas of slip should be carried out as quickly as possible because the slip will make the other clay soft again. Prolonged handling may therefore result in the ware losing shape or even collapsing. Pressmould dishes can be slipped in the mould as soon as they are made and left for support.

2  Take some contrasting slip either on a brush, in a slip trailer or on the finger ends and drop it in blobs on the wet slip surface. If another colour is required, repeat this action.

3  Then holding the bowl or dish in a vertical position, shake downwards in sharp, single movements. The slips will start to run and mingle together.

By turning the ware around at intervals the slip can be forced along different courses until a satisfactory marble effect is achieved (see Fig. 66). Do not overwork the slips or they will merge together as one colour.

Once the ware has been slipped, care should be taken not to touch the surface, otherwise the quality of the smooth finish will be lost.

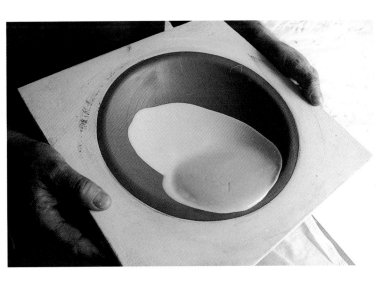

■ Fig. 65. Applying a coat of slip to a pressmoulded dish.

**4** Any unwanted slip can be removed from the rim of the ware with a surform blade when both are leather hard. The edge can then be lightly sponged or allowed to dry out and then smoothed with wire wool (beware of causing dust).

# Sgraffito ('scratched')

This is a method of decoration in which the design is scratched through a film of slip to reveal the contrasting colour of the clay beneath. This scratching technique can also be used on pigments and glazes.

Sgraffito has been a popular method of decoration from the eleventh- and twelfth-century Byzantine ware to the exciting pottery made by the modern Pueblo Indian tribes of New Mexico. The precision and detail in the decoration of some of these sgraffito wares illustrates the sharp contrast between this method and the chance happenings of marbling.

Sgraffito is really a development of incising, although the cutting need only be deep enough to remove the film of slip. The same tools used for incising will do for sgraffito and the cutting is done when slip and clay are leather hard.

It is possible to do sgraffito work on dry clay with a fine pointed tool, but at this stage there is a tendency for the slip to chip. In addition to shaped bamboo or cane, a nail file with a point at one end and a wider round shape at the other is a useful sgraffito tool. The sharp edges of the nail file give a clean cut in leather hard clay. The method of sgraffito is as follows:

■ Fig. 67. Sgraffito decoration

**1** Slip the ware as explained in 'marbling'. For vessel shapes the slip is applied by dipping the ware into the slip. It is usual to slip only the outside of the ware. All-over slipping would cause the ware to become very soft and lose shape or even collapse. The slip should, of course, be of a contrasting colour to the clay.

**2** When the slip and ware are leather hard, lightly mark out the design on the surface of the slip. Then with either the bamboo or nail file, cut through the slip to reveal the contrasting clay beneath (see Fig. 67). If there should be any 'burring' on the edge of the cut, this can be dusted off with the finger when the ware is dry.

# Slip trailing

This is the method of applying a slip decoration by squeezing thickish slip from a rubber bulb or bag through some sort of nozzle. There are a variety of slip trailers on the market. Points to note when choosing or making a trailer are that it must be easy to fill, permit an even flow of liquid and be easy to clean. I have found that the rubber bulb with a detachable plastic nozzle meets all these requirements.

While slip can be trailed on vessel shapes, it is much easier to work on flat ware. Slip can be trailed directly on to damp, firm ware or on to a wet coating of slip. It can be trailed in blobs or lines (see Fig. 68). Illustrations of many slip-trailing techniques can be seen in the work of the seventeenth- and eighteenth-century English slipware potters of which the huge 'Toft' dishes are an outstanding example.

■ Fig. 68. Slip-trailed decoration.

## Combing

This is a technique which can be used in conjunction with slip trailing on a wet slip surface. The comb is blunt toothed and is made of wood, leather or rubber. It is used for moving the slips about into a design. Combing can also be done on a plain, wet slipped surface to reveal the contrasting clay beneath.

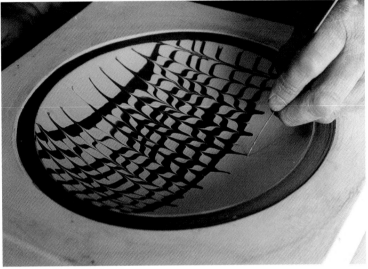

■ Fig. 69. Feather-combed decoration.

## Feather combing

Traditional 'feathering' is the drawing of a fine point or sharpened quill across parallel lines of slip which have been trailed on to a wet slip background of a contrasting colour. By alternating the procedure first one way and then the other, a traditional pattern can be produced (see Fig. 69 above). The fine point should not be dug into the slip but lightly drawn across its surface. Many variations of drawing slip out from trailed lines can be produced with a bit of imagination.

Trailed slip will tend to be in relief to the rest of the surface. This is a characteristic of the method. If, however, the relief is too raised, a light tapping or jolting of the ware should level the slip out.

# Resist

This form of decoration is when the poured or dipped slip is prevented from adhering to the design areas on the ware. The slip should again be of a contrasting colour to the ware and adhesion is prevented in one of the following ways.

## Wax resist

This involves painting the positive or negative design on the ware using molten candle wax thinned with paraffin. The paraffin will help the candle wax adhere to the raw clay and should be mixed in a proportion of three parts wax to one part paraffin. The wax is melted in a metal container (tin can) in a pan of boiling water. This is so that the wax will remain in a molten state for some time, should it be necessary to remove it from the heat. The wax is then freely applied to the ware with a brush which should then be kept for this purpose. When the slip is applied, either by pouring or dipping, it will run off the waxed areas. The wax then burns away in the firing. Make sure that the wax has adhered to the clay surface before applying the slip. Any loose wax will wash away in the flow of slip which will then have to be sieved again before use.

An emulsion wax resist is available from potters' merchants and can be applied straight from the bottle. However, this has never worked as well for me as liquid candle wax. I have used Copydex (latex adhesive) with some success. This dries to a rubbery solid which can be removed like an elastic band when the applied slip is leather hard.

## Stencil resist

In this method the negative or positive design is cut out of thin paper which is then stuck on to the damp ware. Plain newsprint is excellent for this purpose and should be secured to the clay surface by dabbing with a damp sponge. The slip is then applied as before. When this has dried leather hard, the paper can carefully be removed exposing the resist decoration.

■ Stoneware bowls.

# Slip painting

This is simply the method of applying slip decoration with a brush. The most suitable type of brush for slip painting is thick, soft and pointed. It should be kept well loaded with slip while painting, as too thin an application can result in loss of colour when fired. The brush will leave a lined texture in the slip which can be regarded as part of the technique. While slip painting is usually done on leather hard ware, a thinner application can be used on dry ware, but the risk of cracking or peeling, due to different shrinkage rates, is obviously increased. Bands of slip can be applied using a flat-ended brush and bench whirler or banding wheel. If the form is circular the loaded brush is held lightly against it and the wheel gently spun. While this obviously cannot be done with angular

■ Porcelain teapots with slip inlaid decoration.

shapes, it is easier to band them on the whirler than on the bench. Bands of slip are usually used as a ground for one of the other methods of decoration such as sgraffito.

Another process of brushed slip is called 'pâte-sur-pâte'. This method, while not at present popular, is nevertheless of some interest. The design is built up in different thicknesses of porcelain slip. The colours are usually white on a dark background giving different degrees of relief and translucency depending on the thickness of the slip. The method was introduced into England in 1870 by a Frenchman called Marc Louis Solon (pseudonym 'Miles') when he joined the firm of Minton's.

Further information about slips and their colouring agents is given on page 14.

# Underglaze painting

This is the method of painting designs in pigment on to a dry clay surface. The pigment is then 'fixed' in the biscuit firing and will show through a transparent glaze. The colours may also be applied to biscuit ware but have to be mixed with a gum solution (arabic or tragacanth) or a commercial underglaze medium to prevent them from running when the glaze is applied. The first method is therefore the best for the following reasons:

■ The powdered underglaze colour has simply to be mixed with water (proportions can be decided only by experience). Using a gum arabic solution or underglaze medium instead of just water does however help adhesion and prevent smudging.
■ The colour can easily be removed if a mistake is made, using a metal scraper and wire wool.
■ The colour is fixed in the biscuit firing so cannot run when the glaze is applied.

Underglaze colours are made from various blends of metallic oxides, flux to make them sinter and refractory materials to prevent them running or blurring under the glaze. These are then calcined into a hard mass and then finely ground. While it is possible to make one's own colours, it is rather an unnecessary labour. Commercial colours are much better and cheaper in the long run. These colours are tested and the recommended firing temperature given, so that the colour is not appreciably changed or lost by overfiring. Some colours will, however, fire to 1280°C without fading. The necessary gum medium can also be purchased, ready prepared, if the biscuit stage application is required.

■ Resist decoration.

Underglaze colours can be mixed in palettes of the type used for mixing powder paints or ground to a finer consistency with a palette knife or a glazed tile and can be applied with a variety of brushes. As with slip painting, lines or circular bands of colour can be applied with the use of the whirler or banding wheel.

Conditions which will vary the basic shades of underglaze colours are:

- Their degree of thickness when applied.
- The temperature to which they are fired.
- The background on which they are painted. (The brightest results are achieved on a light background. A dark background will give a much quieter but often very pleasant effect.)
- The colour of the transparent glaze which is put over them. For example, under a clear glaze the underglaze colours will remain more or less unchanged while under a yellow transparent glaze, blue will appear green.

# Burnishing

This is not so much a method of decoration but more a finish to the clay surface. Burnishing was the method of lessening the porosity of the fired ware before the discovery of glaze. This type of pottery finish is said to have been used in the Near East before 5000 BC. With the development of glazes the original need for burnishing has been removed, but the aesthetic qualities still remain important. Coiled and pinched ware are often well suited to this type of finish. Indeed the very beautiful and highly decorated wares of the Pueblo Indians of New Mexico are still finished in this way.

Burnishing is carried out at the leather hard stage. The finish is achieved by rubbing the clay surface with some smooth hard object using a circular action (Fig. 12). A smooth pebble, bone or even the back of an old toothbrush or spoon handle have proved successful burnishing tools.

There are really two types of clay surface which can be burnished. These are:

- The plain leather hard surface of the ware.
- A surface which has been slipped with a very highly refined clay and allowed to dry leather hard. This surface will take a higher polish than the first and can be coloured.

Clay which has been sufficiently burnished should retain the polish after firing. The firing, however, must be on the soft side or the polish will be lost. Temperatures around 1000°C can be tried as a starter and decreased if the burnish fires out. The Pueblo Indians' pottery is generally fired at between 800°C to 900°C. Polishing after firing with a soft dry cloth can often improve a dulled surface.

I would like to mention at this point that, in the interests of hygiene, any surface which is going to come into contact with food or the mouth, should be glazed. The glazed pot should then be fired to a sufficient temperature to eliminate the risk of poisoning through metal release. This, however, is fully explained in the next chapter.

## Summary

While I have listed each method of decoration separately, using one method in conjunction with another can often achieve a more interesting or aesthetic result. For example, sgraffito and paper resists, or underglaze painting on a coloured slip (dry surface).

Finally, texturing a surface using the impress method has already been suggested. However, many interesting textures can be obtained by an imaginative use of miscellaneous tools. A broken hacksaw blade, a fork or an old comb are all worth experimenting with.

# 5

# Glazes

A glaze is a thin, glassy coating melted on the surface of a pot to make it non-porous and of the required colour and texture.

Glaze is not, by any means, a modern addition to pottery-making. Alkaline glazes were being used in Egypt around 5000 BC. These invariably peeled off or fell off the pot and it was not until the Mesopotamian discovery of a lead glaze, around 2000 BC, that this fault was overcome.

While modern glazes are similar in many ways to those of ancient times, a fuller understanding of the workings of a glaze has to some extent given the modern potter more control over the materials.

I do not propose to overwhelm the beginner with long explanations as to what a glaze is in chemical terms. This seems to me to be out of the realm of the artist potter and into the field of the chemist. However, as already stated in Chapter 1, it is essential to know something of the nature of the materials with which one is working if their full potential is to be realized. While good glazes can be purchased from the supplier and require little knowledge as to their use, half the excitement of pottery-making is producing an individual finish, however slight.

■ Left: Porcelain perfume bottle.

## The nature of a glaze

The main components of a glaze, silica and alumina, are similar to those of clay. The difference lies in the proportions of these components and the temperature to which they are fired. A glaze does not necessarily need alumina, and the reasons for its inclusion or omission will be discussed at a later stage. Silica is therefore the primary oxide of a glaze. If it is heated to a temperature of 1710°C it will melt, and at this temperature it is a clear liquid. When it cools, it sets or freezes into an extremely hard, durable, non-crystalline solid. A more familiar illustration of this state of matter is with water. Above 0°C water is a liquid, while below 0°C it becomes a solid. However to melt silica at 1710°C is impractical and difficult in most kilns so its melting temperature has to be lowered. This is done by the addition of a flux or melting agent. The simple formula for a glaze would therefore read:

$$silica + flux = glaze$$

Alumina can be added to this formula in small quantities to prevent the glaze from crystallizing on cooling; for while silica does not crystallize, some of the fluxing agents might. These then are the components of a clear, transparent, shiny glaze to which one can add matting agents, opacifiers and colouring oxides or stains as required. A fuller explanation of glaze materials is necessary before this can be done.

# Materials for making glazes

## Silica

This, as stated, is the primary ingredient of a glaze. Other ingredients added to the silica are fluxes (to lower its melting-point) and agents to introduce colour, mattness, opacity and alkalinity if any of these properties are required. As will be explained later, alkalinity is necessary in some glazes to produce certain colour effects.

The proportion of silica to other glaze materials is as follows:

- In glazes which mature at 1080°C or less (low fired or soft glaze), 2 parts silica to 1 part other glaze materials.
- In glazes which mature at 1250°C or above (high fired or hard glaze), 4 parts silica to 1 part other glaze materials.

The proportions of silica are variable between these two extremes.

At the level at which this book is written, these facts are important only in as much as they will help the beginner to understand the following points:

- Why high-fired glazes are harder and more durable than low-fired glazes. This is because of the higher temperature; they can contain a higher silica to flux ratio.
- Why some glazes melt at a lower temperature than others. This is because their flux to silica ratio is higher.

Pure silica is added to the glaze mixture in the form of powdered flint or quartz. Clay and felspar also contain silica, a fact which has to be taken into account when glaze recipes are compiled.

## Alumina

This is a highly refractory material with a melting temperature of 2040°C. It is generally added in small quantities to glazes for the following reasons:

- To give stiffness or viscosity to the melted glaze, thus preventing it from running off vertical surfaces.
- To prevent the devitrification of some of the glaze ingredients during cooling.
- To increase the hardness, durability and mechanical strength.
- To give a matting effect. The degree of mattness would, of course, depend on how much alumina was used and the temperature to which the glaze was fired.

The alumina content of a glaze should, however, be reduced or even omitted if certain effects are required, for example, the production of a strong turquoise glaze or the encouragement of a crystalline one.

Alumina is best purchased as calcined alumina rather than alumina hydrate. This is because it is more concentrated in this form and has no chemically combined water which can impair glaze adhesion during the early stages of firing. Generally, alumina is introduced into glazes in the form of clays with a high alumina content such as ball clay or china clay.

## The fluxing agents

The following oxides make up the rest of the clear glaze formula providing the melting power. Some oxides are stronger fluxes then others and often more than one flux is used in a glaze. All have their individual characteristics and purposes which are as follows:

## Barium oxide (toxic)

This is a refractory material but is used as a secondary flux in high-temperature glazes in quantities up to 10% of the whole. In quantities of around 20%, it produces a satin matt surface. It gives a good alkali colour response and in the presence of boron gives a free-flowing glaze with a glossy finish. It is introduced into the glaze mixture as barium carbonate.

## Boric oxide

This oxide is a strong flux and can be used in low and high-temperature glazes. It intensifies the effect of the colouring oxides in a similar way to sodium and potassium. However, it also has the advantage of reducing the thermal expansion of a glaze by forming borates, thus increasing the resistance to crazing.

Boric oxide can be introduced into glaze mixtures either in the form of colemanite (calcium borate or boro calcite) in which it is insoluble, or as borax frit.

## Calcium oxide

This is perhaps the most commonly used flux in high-temperature glazes. In low-temperature glazes it is used in conjunction with other fluxes such as lead to give the glaze hardness and durability. In large quantities (30–50%) it has a dulling effect, particularly in low- temperature glazes.

Calcium oxide is introduced into the glaze mixture as calcium carbonate or whiting (crushed chalk).

## Lead oxide (toxic)

Lead oxide can be used in temperatures up to 1200°C. Above this limit it becomes volatile. Lead oxide has undoubtedly been the most used fluxing agent since its first known use in Mesopotamia around 2000 BC. Lead oxide will produce a glaze by itself, combining with the silica of the clay. English medieval potters used this type of glaze, applying the dry powdered lead ore (galena) by putting it into a bag with an open weave and then shaking the powder on to the leather hard ware. The ware was then given a single firing in which the pot and glaze matured in one operation.

Lead oxide gives a good colour response to the colouring oxides and having a low coefficient of expansion, helps to resist crazing. Its inclusion in a glaze mixture usually produces a trouble-free finish if properly fired.

However, there is a big disadvantage to using lead oxide in its raw state, which is that it is poisonous and potentially dangerous in this form.

Lead poisoning can result from inhaling the dust or by carelessly getting glaze into the mouth via cigarettes, etc. The problem of lead poisoning became so severe in the English pottery industry that lead is no longer used in its raw state but in a fritted form (see 'frit', page 73). The use of raw lead is obviously not allowed in schools or colleges of education. Fritted lead has much the same effect and is non-poisonous.

For potters experienced enough to use it, lead oxide might still be available from suppliers in the form of lead carbonate (white lead), lead oxide (Litharge, yellow lead), lead oxide (red lead), lead sulphide (galena, black lead), the latter being insoluble. However, it is much safer to use lead frit which can be purchased as lead bisilicate and lead sesquisilicate.

## Lithium oxide

This oxide is introduced into alkaline glaze mixtures as lithium carbonate. It is an active flux, insoluble, and has a similar colour response to potassium and sodium. It is more expensive than the latter but has a lower coefficient of expansion (see Glossary) thus reducing the risk of crazing.

## Magnesium oxide

This oxide is a high-temperature flux and is introduced into glazes as magnesium carbonate. It produces a smooth, semi-matt surface if used in quantities of up to 10% of the whole. Larger quantities than this would make the glaze dry and opaque, with the possibility of pin- holing and crawling (see the section on glaze faults on page 90). Interesting colour effects can be obtained if it is used in combination with cobalt and manganese.

When both the oxides of magnesium and calcium are required in a glaze, they can be introduced in the form of dolomite. This is a natural material in which

■ Porcelain bowl thrown and slabbed.

magnesium and calcium occur as carbonates in equal parts. Magnesia and silica can be introduced into glazes and clays as talc (french chalk, magnesium silicate).

## Potassium oxide

In glazes, this oxide reacts similarly to sodium oxide with which it is found in insoluble form in the mineral felspar (see page 6, Felspar).

Potassium oxide or potash is an alkaline substance giving a brilliant colour response in glazes. It has a high coefficient of expansion and if used in large quantities will cause crazing. If, however, the colour response is more important than the crazing and large quantities of potash are required, it is best introduced into the glaze as a manufactured frit rather than felspar.

While pearl ash (potassium carbonate) and nitre (potassium nitrate) are a source of potassium, they are soluble and are generally used in the manufacture of frit.

## Sodium oxide

In glazes sodium oxide reacts similarly to potassium, being a strong flux and giving brilliance to the colouring oxides. Sodium oxide has a higher coefficient of expansion than potassium oxide with the result that glazes of high soda content tend to craze.

The main source of sodium oxide is soda ash (sodium carbonate). This is soluble and is usually used in the manufacture of a frit.

## Strontium oxide

This is a high-temperature flux and is added to the glaze mixture as strontium carbonate. However, as its function in a glaze is similar to that of calcium, and it is dearer, it is little used.

The above, then, are the oxides used for fluxing the silica and from which all clear glazes are made. But, before continuing with the development of glazes any further, some items need a little more explanation. These are toxicity, solubility and frit.

## Toxicity

Most pottery materials are quite safe in use. There are some which are toxic and these I have indicated in the text. There is absolutely nothing to worry about when using these materials so long as the following common sense points are observed:

- Do not smoke or consume food or drink while handling these materials.
- Do not use these materials in dusty or draughty conditions.
- Protective clothing should be changed before eating or drinking, etc.
- Hands should be washed thoroughly after using these materials, and certainly before eating or drinking.

## Solubility

Materials which dissolve in water are said to be soluble. This is a disadvantage in glaze-making for the following reasons:

- There is a risk of unbalancing the glaze by losing some dissolved material if any of the water is lost. It also prevents thickening the glaze by allowing the solids to settle and then draining off some of the surplus water.
- It is difficult to keep the glaze in good condition when not in use because it has a tendency to go lumpy.
- Some soluble materials absorb moisture from the atmosphere (are hygroscopic) and are therefore difficult to keep dry in storage.

## A frit

This is the resultant glass when water-soluble materials are melted with silica to obtain low melting silicates. These are then not soluble in water.

The method of making a frit is easy in theory but a little more difficult in practice, largely because of the equipment needed to produce a sufficiently powdered material for adding to a glaze mixture. Also making one's own frit defeats part of the purpose of using a frit in the first place; which is to avoid using very toxic materials like lead oxide. It is, therefore, better to buy frits already prepared from the potters' merchant.

Nevertheless it is of interest to know the method of making a frit which is as follows:

- The materials are weighed out and placed in a crucible.
- They are then heated in a kiln or furnace until melted.
- While the frit is in a molten state the crucible is removed from the heat and the contents poured into cold water. The sudden freezing of the frit shatters it into small pieces which are then ground to a fine powder in a ball mill.

# Types of glazes and glaze recipes

While all base glazes are compiled from various combinations and proportions of the oxides already listed, there has to be more than one type of glaze for the following reasons:

- To cope with the wide temperature range from the lowest fired earthenware at around 850°C to the highest fired stoneware and porcelain at 1350°C+.
- To give different colour effects.
- To give different surface qualities.

Glazes, like clays, are rather difficult to group because the categories sometimes overlap. For convenience, however, a grouping can be made according to the nature of the fluxing agent or the temperature at which the glaze matures. These are:

*Soft or low-temperature glazes* (maturing at 1080°C or below)

  **earthenware** (alkaline, lead, boracic ) *fritted* – those made from fritted materials and therefore insoluble in water.

*Hard or high-temperature glazes* (maturing at 1250°C or above)

  **stoneware, porcelain** (felspathic, ash) *raw* – those made from raw unfritted materials generally soluble in water.

## Alkaline glazes

These are glazes which are fluxed by the alkalies potassium, sodium or lithium. They are low temperature glazes maturing below 1080°C due to the high proportion of alkaline fluxes.

The characteristics of this type of glaze are:

- Strong colour response with the colouring oxides, notably turquoise with copper oxide.
- Shiny surface with a tendency to run at melting-point. A small addition of alumina would correct this but tends to spoil the colour response. Copper would become green rather than turquoise.
- Softness (easily scratched).
- Likely to craze. This is due to the high coefficient of expansion of the fluxes. An alkaline glaze would therefore be used for its colour effects rather than for its durability or reliability. Also because it tends to craze and is slightly soluble in the presence of weak acids, it is not suitable for ware intended to contain food or drink.

The following is a recipe which I have successfully used to obtain a strong turquoise with copper:

|  | % (by weight) |
|---|---|
| alkaline frit | 74 |
| felspar | 15 (fire to 1050°C) |
| flint or quartz | 11 |

## Lead glazes

Fluxed by some form of lead oxide (preferably fritted), these glazes are the ones most generally used on earthenware pottery. Maturing from temperatures of around 860°C to 1200°C, they give the potter plenty of scope in the earthenware range.

The characteristics of a lead glaze are mostly to the potter's advantage, these being:

- Good colour response, though not as vivid as in alkaline glazes. Copper gives green rather than turquoise.
- Reliability in firing.
- Bright, smooth, shiny surface.
- Durability if fired in the 1050°–1150°C temperature range.

This type of glaze can therefore be recommended for its versatility in the temperature range stated and has a good food surface if submitted to fire above 1050°C using the bisilicate frit. The following is a suggested recipe:

|  | % (by weight) |  |
| --- | --- | --- |
| lead bisilicate | 57 | |
| felspar | 31 | (fire to 1080°C) |
| whiting | 5 | |
| china clay | 7 | |

## Boracic glazes

These are glazes where the main fluxing agent is boric oxide. Used mainly in the same temperature range as lead glazes, they provide an alternative standard lead-free glaze. The characteristics are slightly different from the lead glaze and are as follows:

- Strong colour response, more like alkaline than lead glaze, i.e. copper gives a green turquoise, with better craze resistance.
- Tends to be milky if applied too thickly or slightly underfired.

Boracic glazes are fluxed with borax frit or, in the case of higher temperature glazes, with colemanite (calcium borate or boro calcite). The latter is a natural insoluble source of boric oxide. The following is a suggested recipe for this type of glaze:

|  | % (by weight) |  |
| --- | --- | --- |
| borax frit | 28 | |
| felspar | 22 | |
| whiting | 11 | (fire to 1080°C) |
| china clay | 15 | |
| flint | 23 | |
| Bentonite | 1 | |

## Felspathic stoneware and porcelain glazes

These glazes mature at high temperatures in the range of 1200°C to 1350°C and are similar in composition. They are generally fluxed with felspar of one kind or another, this being the main ingredient.

Felspar melts by itself at approximately 1260°C and in theory contains all the ingredients of a glaze for that temperature, these being silica, alumina, soda, potash or lime. In practice, more suitable stoneware glazes can be made if these oxides are adjusted by adding small quantities of china clay (alumina), quartz (silica) and whiting (calcium).

## Ash stoneware glazes

Wood or plant ash contains the necessary oxides for a stoneware glaze melting at around 1260°C, but like felspar it is better if these oxides are adjusted. Also, like felspar, these ashes vary in composition and fusibility, some containing more silica than others and therefore being more refractory. The thing to do is to try a selection of ashes from a known source and keep a careful record (as with all glaze experiments) listing the type of ash, the glaze and the results. Autumn is the time to look for ash from the debris of garden bonfires, along hedgerows or in cornfields. Also bits of wood or plants can be collected, the type noted, and

■ Stoneware bowls.

then burned in a clean place out of the wind. A lot of wood is required to produce a small amount of ash. If it is not possible to produce one's own ash, Potclays supply wood ash which is unsieved and unwashed. Before ash is of any use in glazes it has to be washed and sieved. The method of preparing ash for a glaze is as follows:

■ Mix the ash with a quantity of water and pass this mixture through an 80 mesh sieve to remove unburnt material.

■ Allow the sieved ash to settle and then pour off the water to remove soluble materials.

■ Add fresh water and repeat the process, this time sieving through 120 mesh.

■ Allow the solids to settle, pour off the water and allow the ash to dry. The ash is then ready for use in the glaze mixture.

Ash glazes usually rely on the subtle colours given by the small amount of natural pigment in them. They

can, however, be further coloured by adding small amounts of colouring oxides which are listed later on in this section. Ash glazes should also be fired in a reducing atmosphere (see Firing) if their colour is to be fully developed.

The following are suggested recipes for three high temperature glazes:

| Stoneware glaze | % (by weight) | Porcelain glaze | % (by weight) |
|---|---|---|---|
| felspar | 48 | china stone | 20 |
| whiting | 20 | whiting | 23 |
| china clay | 22 | china clay | 30 |
| flint | 10 | quartz | 27 |
| (fire to 1250°C+) | | (fire to 1280°C) | |

| Ash glaze | % (by weight) |
|---|---|
| ash | 40 |
| felspar | 40 |
| china clay | 20 |
| (fire to 1250°C (oxidizing or reducing)) | |

N.B. The maturing temperature and quality of an ash glaze will depend largely on the type of ash used, and the atmosphere in the kiln.

High temperature glazes have a beauty all their own. This is perhaps because they are quieter in colour and less shiny than the soft earthenware glazes, thus retaining much of the clay-made quality. I have often thought how much more attractive some ware seems when it is first cut from the wheel than when it is completed. This is surely because, in the glazing, the natural quality of the clay has been disregarded and drowned in colour and shine. Stoneware glazes also have the practical advantages of being very hard, very durable and resistant to acid attack.

The above, then, are base clear or semi-clear glazes suitable for application to plain or decorated biscuit ware, so long as the pot and glaze match one another at the correct maturing temperature. These base glazes can be coloured; made opaque; matted or adjusted to give certain effects or finish. Let us therefore proceed step by step.

# Colouring agents

Base glazes are coloured by the addition of small quantities of certain metallic oxides. In the following list I will give a general description of the colour properties of these oxides and suggest the quantities and combinations in which they may be added. This, however, can only be used as a guide because so much depends on the thickness of the glaze, the colour of the pot (clay) to which it is applied, the temperature to which it is fired and the atmosphere in the kiln.

But in many ways it is this uncertainty of the result that creates much of the excitement in studio pottery.

N.B. The percentages given for adding colouring agents to glazes or slips are outside percentages. That is to say 100% of glaze plus the outside percentage of colouring agent, e.g. 100% (parts) of glaze plus 10% (parts) of colouring agent making 110% (parts) of mixture in all.

## Antimonate of lead (toxic)

This is a valuable yellow stain which in proportions of up to 10% in a lead glaze will give the traditional Naples yellow. In leadless glazes it is not very stable. With a small quantity of iron oxide it will give orange tints. Suggested quantities for adding to a glaze: up to 10%.

## Chromium oxide (toxic)

This oxide gives a variety of colour, depending on the base glaze and the maturing temperature. Generally 2% of chrome gives a green. In low-fired lead glazes below 950°C and containing no soda, an orange red can be produced. With 1% of chrome, a brilliant yellow can be developed in lead glazes containing soda. In the presence of tin oxide, a pink colour

usually results. This is often the most annoying characteristic of chrome oxide for, in a kiln full of white tin glazed pots, a small amount of volatile chrome will turn them all an unpleasant pink. Suggested quantities for adding to a glaze: 1–3%.

## Cobalt oxide (toxic)

This is the most powerful colouring oxide, giving strong blues in quantities of up to 1.5%. Cobalt has also a strong fluxing effect on glazes and, like certain other colouring oxides, can lower their maturing temperatures. This is something to be aware of when colouring a glaze. The blue of cobalt ranges from an inky blue in both lead and leadless glazes to a vivid blue in alkaline glazes. In the presence of magnesium the colour is more purple. Cobalt oxide gives speckled blues while the carbonate form, being finer grained, gives a more even distribution of colour. Suggested quantities for adding to a glaze: up to 1.5%.

## Copper oxide (toxic)

This is a most versatile pigment and along with iron oxide is perhaps the most useful. Added in quantities of up to 5%, copper oxide gives a green colour in lead glazes much pleasanter than chrome. In an alkaline glaze, without alumina, 2% of copper will give a brilliant turquoise. In reduction firings (see Firing), 1% of copper oxide plus a little tin oxide will produce a red colour. In quantities of 5–10% copper will produce a metallic black in any glaze. The carbonate form will produce a more even distribution of colour. Suggested quantities for adding to a glaze: up to 5%.

## Iron oxide

This is perhaps the most used colouring oxide in pottery, giving shades of amber, reddy brown, greens, blues, greys and blacks, depending on the quantity used, the firing temperature and the kiln conditions. Being the natural colouring agent of many clays, iron oxide often seems the most suitable pigment to use for both staining glazes and over-glaze painting. It also

■ Thrown stoneware with oxide decoration.

■ Thrown earthenware with oxide decoration.

modifies the shades of other pigments and has a certain amount of fluxing power. It can be purchased in a variety of forms as can be seen from any merchant's catalogue. The one most generally used is red iron oxide, which in quantities of up to 5% will give ambers in lead glazes. Up to 2% will give celadon greens in stoneware reductions and 10% will give black in stoneware reduction. Crocus martis, a natural ferric oxide, will give speckled effects, as will iron spangles; while iron chromate (1–3%) will give greys. Suggested quantities for adding to a glaze: up to 10%.

### Manganese oxide

Generally used in the form of manganese dioxide (black), this oxide is a very active flux, giving browns in most glazes. However, in alkaline glazes a purple or plum colour can be obtained, particularly in

combination with a little tin oxide. For a more even distribution of colour, manganese carbonate can be used. Suggested quantities for adding to a glaze: 1–6%.

### Nickel oxide (toxic)

This oxide has been little used as a pigment, perhaps because of its uncertainty of colour. It tends to produce grey in lead glazes, tan in the presence of calcium, bright green in high magnesium glazes and a grey blue with zinc. It is usually used to modify other colours. Suggested quantities for adding to a glaze: 1–3%.

### Vanadium oxide (toxic)

This oxide can be purchased as vanadium pentoxide which is usually used in conjunction with tin oxide to produce an opaque yellow. Suggested quantities for adding to a glaze: 4–10%.

## Glaze stains

These are commercially prepared colours which, in addition to staining glazes, are often suitable for staining slips, underglaze painting and painting on to unfired glaze. The manufacturer's instructions should be carefully studied to see what is claimed for each colour. These colours are made from the colouring oxides listed, which are calcined with other materials to bring out their colouring properties. Suggested quantities for adding to a glaze: 4–8%.

These, then, are the main colouring agents. There are a few more, but they are so expensive or difficult to obtain that their inclusion seems pointless. Of the oxides listed, the main ones are undoubtedly cobalt, copper, iron and manganese. An understanding of these is therefore of prime importance to the potter.

The most interesting colours are usually obtained by combining two or three oxides together in a glaze. The oxides are added in small quantities of up to 10% in all. Some colouring oxides are much stronger than others, therefore one should start experimenting with very small quantities, for example, 100 parts of transparent lead glaze plus one part cobalt plus two parts iron will give a dark green. Also remember that on dark biscuit pots, the coloured glazes, if very transparent, will appear as various shades of brown or black.

To the list of colouring pigments must be added the metal oxides which make a glaze white and opaque. The degree of opacity and whiteness depends on the type and amount of opacifier used, the type of glaze in which it is used, the thickness of the applied glaze, and in some cases the colour of the biscuit ware.

## Tin oxide

This is the most widely used and effective opacifier giving a 'quiet' white. For semi-opacity use 5%, and for complete opacity, use 10%. Thick tin glaze tends to crawl (see page 91).

## Titanium oxide

This oxide gives a creamy or buff opacity with a semi-matt surface in quantities of 5–10%.

Rutile and Ilmenite are natural sources of titanium, but contain a varying amount of iron oxide which gives a tan colour to glazes in which they are used. As well as increasing opacity, their main use in glazes is to give speckles or develop glaze texture. They are usually added to glazes in quantities of 2–6%.

## Zinc oxide (toxic)

In quantities of 10–15% this oxide produces opacity, mattness and dryness of texture. It has an interesting effect on other colours in glazes, particularly blues. In small quantities it is used as a secondary flux in high temperature glazes. However, glazes containing a high quantity of zinc oxide are subject to pitting and pinholing (see page 91) and have a tendency to crawl. As an opacifier it is therefore best used in conjunction with tin or zirconium.

## Zirconium oxide and zirconium silicate (zircon)

These are similar in opacifying powers, producing a harsher, more neutral white than tin in proportions of 10–15%. They have a low expansion and therefore increase craze resistance. Used in equal parts with tin, either will produce a satisfactory opacifier which is cheaper than pure tin.

To white, opaque glazes, one may add small quantities of colouring pigment, if required, with interesting results.

# Other glazes

So far, transparent, coloured and opaque glazes have been described. There are other glaze effects which have some or all of these properties but require further description.

## Matt glazes

These are the glazes which have a 'coarse', non-reflecting surface in contrast to the shiny glazes which have a smooth reflecting surface. The degree of mattness can be varied just like the degree of opacity and these semi-matt glazes are among the most beautiful.

All matt glazes are opaque or semi-opaque, due to their absorption or diffusion of light; but not all opaque glazes are matt. There is a relationship between the two, and while there appear to be different opinions as to what constitutes a true matt glaze and how one should go about obtaining it, a matt glaze results from either of the following:

- Underfiring the glaze by increasing its refractory materials, thus raising its maturing point. An increase in the alumina content of a glaze will produce this type of matt finish.
- Encouraging the glaze to crystallize into small crystals on cooling. This can be done by the addition of calcium oxide (whiting) to the glaze in a proportion of 20%. Titanium oxide in proportions of 5–10% will also give this crystalline mattness.

| matt glaze type (a) | % | matt glaze type (b) |
|---|---|---|
| lead sesquisilicate | 48 | stoneware glaze (already given) |
| felspar | 26 | +5% titanium oxide (rutile) |
| china clay | 16 | +3% zinc oxide |
| whiting | 10 | (mottled matt white) |
| (fire to 1080°C) | | (fire to 1250°C) |

## Crystalline glazes

These are glazes which devitrify on cooling into larger rather than small crystals. They are developed by the addition of 10% titanium oxide or 20% zinc oxide to a leadless glaze. They must contain little or no alumina, as this helps to prevent devitrification, and therefore are rather fluid.

Another type of crystalline glaze is the aventurine glaze in which the devitrification is caused by the high iron content crystallizing on cooling.

In this type of glaze the flux is usually a lead-borax frit. A suggested recipe is as follows:

| | % (by weight) |
|---|---|
| lead sesquisilicate | 38 |
| borax frit | 37 |
| china stone | 15 |
| iron oxide (spangles) | 7 |
| iron chromate | 3 |
| (fire to 1060°C) | |

The full development of the crystals is only possible if the glaze is cooled slowly.

## Pooled glazes

These are usually either alkaline frits, coloured as explained, or crushed coloured glass, which are applied very thickly to hollows in the biscuit ware. The ware is usually for decorative use only and it must be remembered that this type of glaze can only be applied to horizontal depressions. This is because the glaze is so fluid when melted that if applied to vertical surfaces it would run off the pot on to the kiln shelves.

I have had some interesting effects in school projects using pooled glazes. One was in a project developing large tiles, the decoration of which was based on the Moon's surface. Some splendid relief crater-type forms were made, and after firing, these were filled with coloured alkali frit. In another project the coloured frit was used to fill the bottom half inch of some shallow, thickly-thrown dish forms. In a third project some plant forms were developed and finished in a matt light coloured stoneware glaze. The frits were then poured into some of the hollows and the ware given a third firing.

## Black glazes

These glazes are not difficult to make as far as achieving the right colour is concerned. It is just that sometimes their quality is rather unpleasant.

In most earthenware glazes a black can be made by adding a combination of 2–3% of any three of the oxides copper, cobalt, iron and manganese, in a proportion of not more than 10% in all. The addition of from 6–10% of these fluxing as well as colouring oxides may lower the maturing temperature of the glaze. This will therefore have to be taken into account. More than 5% of copper oxide may produce a matt black effect in some low temperature glazes. There are recipes for both low temperature and high temperature blacks:

| | % | | % |
|---|---|---|---|
| lead (frit) glaze (as given) | 100 | medium stoneware (as given) | 100 |
| + | | | |
| copper oxide | 3 | | |
| | | + | |
| iron oxide | 4 | iron | 10 |
| cobalt oxide | 1 | | |
| (fire to 1060°C) | | (fire to 1250°C (reduction)) | |

## Red glazes

Red is a very elusive colour to obtain in glazes. It is easy enough to produce a beautiful, rusty-brown colour with iron, but warm and bright reds are hard to achieve.

The main problem in producing red glazes is not the base glaze itself but the temperature and atmosphere of the kiln. Most bright reds are produced either in a low temperature glaze, in a reducing atmosphere or in both. This takes them out of the general earthenware or stoneware temperatures.

Commercial red glazes are made with cadmium and selenium and are designed to fire at normal earthenware temperatures (about 1040°C). Cadmium and selenium are difficult materials to obtain and

while I have read many accounts of how to produce a red glaze, there seem to be very few red-glazed pots around. Therefore if a red glaze is particularly required, the commercial product might be advisable. For the home researcher, however, there are usually three options for producing a red glaze, and these are:

- Chrome oxide in a high lead glaze (perhaps with a little tin: try 2%). Oxidizing fire.
- Copper oxide plus a little tin oxide in a lead borosilicate glaze. Reducing fire.
- Copper oxide, plus a little tin oxide in a stoneware glaze. Try the medium stoneware glaze given or the soft stoneware glaze listed opposite.

Of these three, the latter is the one that may give the most pleasing red. This particular project is one that will give the researcher plenty of scope. The following recipes are suggested as starters for the three types of red, and good luck!

| glaze (a) | % | glaze (b) | % |
|---|---|---|---|
| lead sesquisilicate | 70 | standard borax frit | 90 |
| china clay | 10 | lead sesquisilicate | 10 |
| flint | 20 | + | |
| + | | tin oxide | 5 |
| chrome oxide | 1 | copper oxide | 1.5 |
| (fire to 960°C oxidizing) | | (fire to 1000°C reducing from 900°C upwards) | |

| glaze (c) | % | |
|---|---|---|
| felspar | 72 | |
| whiting | 13 | (fire to 1230°C reducing) |
| china clay | 7 | |
| flint | 8 | |
| + | | |
| copper oxide | 1.5 | |
| tin oxide | 2 | |

## Raku glaze

Raku pottery is one of the many techniques imported into England from the Orient. It is a technique which was developed by Japanese potters during the sixteenth century to make bowls for the famous 'Tea Ceremony'. Bernard Leach, the father of the present-day tradition of studio potters in Britain, brought the technique back with him on his return from Japan in 1920.

Raku is a type of pottery which one either likes or dislikes. The methods of making it are the same as for most other forms of hand-made pottery, and the principles of firing it are similar but there are two big differences. These are:

- The biscuit firing is low (around 800°C).
- The glaze firing, which is around 860°C, takes only minutes. This is because the kiln is first fired empty to the glaze maturing temperature. Then with the aid of long tongs, the glazed pots are put into the heat, the glaze melted and the pots taken out again to cool.

Raku is therefore a useful teaching technique as it allows one to demonstrate the complete making of a pot very quickly. However, with great respect to the Japanese, I would consider raku as a method of making ornamental pottery rather than ware to use for food and drink. The reasons for this are mainly in the interests of health and hygiene, and are:

- The finished pot must be regarded as porous, due to the soft biscuit and the inevitable crazing of the glaze.
- The soft lead glaze, even with the use of a frit, must be subject to metal release if in contact with acids in food or drink and is therefore a poison risk.

The clay to use for raku should be a heavily grogged stoneware body (30% of 40–60 mesh grog) to withstand the rapid heating and cooling. The ware should also be made of thicker section than other types of pottery. A simple description of raku firing will be given in the chapter on firing and for further details of true raku pottery, reference should be made to Bernard Leach's *A Potter's Book*. It will be seen here that the Japanese raku wares are fired as low as 750°C. Modified recipes for this low-fired ware are as follows:

| | % | | % |
|---|---|---|---|
| lead sesquisilicate | 90 | lead sesquisilicate | 45 |
| flint | 5 | borax frit | 45 |
| china clay | 5 | flint | 5 |
| | | china clay | 5 |

(fire to approx. 880°C)

In these recipes, fritted lead is used instead of white lead, for safety. The glaze can be coloured just the same as any other glaze.

## Salt glaze

This is a glaze produced on stoneware pottery by volatilization (see Glossary) of common salt in the kiln. Salt-glazed stoneware was developed by German potters possibly at Siegburg in the early part of the fifteenth century. The most famous pieces in this type of pottery are probably the jugs and bottles known as 'Bellarmines' (see Glossary). In England the first salt-glazed stoneware is attributed to John Dwight who made his ware at Fulham in the latter half of the seventeenth century.

The glazing is done by introducing moist common salt (sodium chloride) into the kiln fire box or the kiln itself towards the end of the firing. The salt volatilizes into a vapour in which the sodium oxide combines with the silica and alumina of the pot to form a thin coating of glaze. The biscuit and glaze firings are therefore done in one go. Colouring is obtained with the use of coloured engobes or oxides applied to the greenware. A wash of brown engobe was often used to colour the German salt glaze stonewares.

# Glaze mixing

Glaze mixing is quite a straightforward procedure if taken step by step. First, the equipment required is as follows:

- Scales for weighing out the ingredients. There are many varieties available but I have found the beam-type the most useful ones, with a sliding rather than separate weights. The metric scales are the best choice since most weights are now metric and with percentage recipes the weighing-out is easier.
- Pestle and mortar. At one time a pestle and mortar were essential for powdering coarse raw materials. Nowadays, as raw materials are supplied finely ground, these items are really unnecessary. They are, however, still available if required.
- Sieves or lawns. It is necessary to pass the liquid glaze through these to remove coarse particles prior to application. Lawns made with phosphor bronze mesh in beechwood frames are the ones to use. Two lawns are the basic requirement, one of 80 mesh for slips and one of 100 mesh for glazes. These should be washed thoroughly after use. Specks of unwanted colour in clear or white tin glazes are often due to a dirty lawn being used. An extra lawn reserved and marked for clear and white glazes is certainly an asset.
- Glaze containers. A number of polythene buckets with snap-on lids are the most useful of glaze containers. A wide range of sizes can be obtained but I find that the 10-litre (2.2-gallon) bucket is the most useful both for mixing and storing glazes. Dry, raw materials are better stored in polythene bins than in the bags in which they are supplied. Plastic jars with lids are useful for storing oxides, etc. but as I have said before, remember to label each container correctly as to its contents, using a waterproof marker, and then keep the container specifically for that material.
- Bowls and jugs. These items are essential for certain methods of glazing as well as for many other jobs in the pottery.

- Other equipment. There are many small items of equipment which need to be accumulated for glaze mixing, application, and then the cleaning up of the pots. Scoops, funnels, sponges (small natural and large synthetic), wooden spoons or sticks (for stirring the glaze), sticks or thick wire for supporting sieves and pots, lawn brushes, etc. Some of these I have mentioned before but, if possible, it is useful to have a set just for glazes.

As raw materials are generally supplied in powder form, they can simply be weighed out according to the recipe, mixed with water and then sieved. The procedure is as follows:

1  Carefully weigh out the glaze ingredients into a suitable container. A 10-litre (2.2-gallon) bucket will comfortably hold 5.5 kg (approx 200 ounces) of dry material plus water. If there are any lumpy materials these will have to be broken up with the fingers or a pestle and mortar.
2  Add the water to the dry materials and mix. The water content of a glaze can vary depending on:
   (a) the porosity of the biscuit pot (the more porous the pot, the thinner the glaze);
   (b) the type of glaze being mixed.
   Generally, the ratio of water to dry materials is

   3 pint to 172 oz (426 ml to 496 g).

For small quantities of glaze the mixing can be done with a smooth stick or wooden spoon. For larger quantities electric mixers are available from the potters' merchants, complete with plastic tubs. These mixers come in two sizes: 13.6 litre (3 gallon) and 22.8 litre (5 gallon). Jar or ball mills are also used for grinding and mixing glazes. However, as materials become more and more refined, an electric mixer would be a better investment.

I must admit at this point that when mixing glazes by hand I always add the dry materials to an estimated amount of water. The way I have already explained is better in that it cuts down on the amount of dust, which is a health hazard, but tends to make the glaze mixture lumpy and harder to stir. For hand mixing, the material to water method is much easier and by covering your nose and mouth with a dust mask it is possible to protect yourself from the dust.

After the dry material and water have been thoroughly mixed, the liquid should be allowed to stand overnight to allow all the ingredients to break down thoroughly.

3   Pass the liquid glaze through a 100 mesh sieve using a lawn brush or rubber kidney to force it through. There are vibratory machines available to do this job, and while they are relatively expensive to buy, they are cheap to run (see supplier's catalogue). Do not try to force thick glaze through the sieve, just add a little more water to the mix. As the glaze materials used should be insoluble, the water content can always be adjusted later by allowing the materials to settle and then decanting off some of the water.

4   Colouring agents (oxides or stains) can now be added to the glaze if required. They should be weighed out in the correct proportions, mixed with water to a thin consistency in a jug, and then added to the glaze mix. If a speck-free colour is required, the oxide mixture should be passed through a 100–200 mesh cup lawn into the glaze.

5   The glaze, coloured or clear, can now be given a final sieving if this is thought necessary. It is a debatable point how much sieving a glaze or colour agent needs. For a surface coming into contact with food or drink, the smoother the glaze consistency, the better. But for surfaces that are purely for decoration, I have often used a once-sieved glaze and then added the watered colour without any sieving.

6   The glaze should now be allowed to stand for at least 24 hours before use. Letting it stand even longer will improve its quality.

## Glaze suspenders

When not in use, some glazes tend to settle heavily in the bottom of the container. Glazes containing a certain amount of clay do not usually present this problem. As I have already mentioned, 1 to 2% of bentonite added to the dry glaze mix can help solve this problem without affecting the finished glaze. If this does not help it is suggested that a further addition of one or two drops of a saturated solution of calcium chloride be made to each bucket of glaze prior to sieving. This saturated solution is prepared by mixing calcium chloride with a little warm water until no more can be dissolved. When cool, the liquid can be decanted, this being a saturated solution.

# Glaze testing

When researching into new glazes or colour effects, it is always advisable to make up small quantities first, and then to test them before mixing a large batch of glaze. While seeming to be a labour, it will save the time of producing a large quantity of glaze which may be unsatisfactory in finish or colour. Also new batches of a satisfactory glaze should be tested before glazing large quantities of pots.

Testing should be orderly, with the test piece marked and a corresponding reference made in a notebook listing:

■  the glaze recipe
■  thickness of application
■  firing temperature and atmosphere
■  type of pot glazed (clay colour)
■  results.

Miniature bowls and cylindrical shapes are the best ware for testing new glazes on. Miniature tiles are more economical but only give results which are accurate for horizontal ware and, as most glazes are on vertical surfaces, the results can be very misleading. Also, if the glaze is successful, the little bowls are more useful.

# Glaze application

Generally, when applying a glaze the aim is to give the pot an even coating of the correct thickness. This is why the glaze is usually applied in liquid form to the biscuit pot. The water is absorbed by the porous pot, leaving an even coating of powdered glaze deposited on its surface. This is why the amount of water added to the glaze mixture, in other words the consistency of the glaze, should depend largely on the porosity of the biscuit ware. Before actual glazing begins it is a good idea to do a test application on a piece of spare pot similar to the one to be glazed. This will show the thickness of the glaze deposit if the spare pot is subjected to different methods of application for different lengths of time. Hard and fast rules as to the thickness of a glaze deposit are difficult to give. It depends on the type of ware to which the glaze is applied; the colour required; craze resistance; tendency to crawl, etc. Experience is the only successful way of getting to know whether the thickness of the glaze deposit is correct or not. However, a vague guide to thickness may be taken as $\frac{1}{16}$ in. (1.587 mm) thick coating, $\frac{1}{32}$ in. (0.7938 mm) average coating, $\frac{1}{64}$ in. (0.3969 mm) thin coating. The consistency of the liquid glaze should be thin for soft porous biscuit and thicker for hard biscuit. Earthenware pottery usually has a thin coating of glaze, and stoneware a thicker one, but here again trial and error is the usual guide.

There are three main ways of applying glaze. These are: dipping, pouring and spraying.

## Dipping

If one has sufficient glaze in which to submerge the pot comfortably, then this is the most efficient and successful way of applying a glaze. The pot is glazed by quickly dipping it in and out of the mixture. A lengthy submergence would result in a very porous pot being too thickly coated and a less porous pot being saturated with water, thus causing the glaze to be washed off again.

Before applying glaze, no matter what method is used, one should make sure that the surface of the pot is as free from dust and grease as it can be. Both dust and grease would repel the glaze or cause it to crawl (see page 91).

Grease on the pot has to be prevented rather than cured. It usually comes from too much handling of the biscuit ware, particularly in cases where people use hand cream. Therefore biscuit pots should be picked up as little as possible. Dust can be removed by

■ Fig. 70. Holding a jug ready for dipping.

blowing and then wiping the surface of the pot with a damp sponge. Dampening the pot before glaze application will also temporarily reduce porosity.

Before dipping takes place, the glaze should be thoroughly stirred and poured into a container large enough to hold the pot comfortably. The glaze bucket or container itself will be big enough for average-sized, closed-necked pots but for wider bowls and dishes the glaze will have to be transferred to a wider container, such as a plastic bowl. If the glaze is not of a smooth consistency, passing it through an 80-mesh sieve should correct this. Most of the preparatory work is common sense, and is not half as laborious as it may sound.

The technique of dipping will vary, depending on the shape of the pot, but the general procedure is as follows:

1   For small shapes, hold firmly between finger and thumb of one hand, either spanning the rim, or with thumb on the rim and finger underneath (Fig. 70). For larger bowl shapes, four-finger support will be necessary using two fingers of each hand on either side of the rim (see Fig. 72). Pots should be held firmly but with as little finger contact as possible, thus reducing the need for touching up later.

2   Slide the pot through the glaze taking it in and out in one movement. For cylinder shapes, make sure that the glaze gets inside the pot. Trapped air pockets can often prevent glaze getting in. This can sometimes be made use of (see Combination glazes on page 83).

3   Hold the pot upside down and shake once (Fig. 71).

4   Place the pot, the right way up, on a stilt or spurs (see Fig. 75) to dry.

■ Fig. 72. Support the bowl using two fingers of each hand on either side of the rim.

5   Touch up contact marks with either a soft brush or a finger loaded with glaze. These marks, or any dribbles, can be carefully rubbed smooth when the glaze has dried. This is particularly necessary in the case of matt glazes, as these are not very fluid in the molten stage and so do not even out. The glaze is usually cleaned from the base of stoneware pots (see Cleaning up).

## Pouring

This method is used when the pot is too large for dipping or when there is not enough glaze. Pouring can also be used for glazing the inside of a vessel when a contrasting or different glaze is required on the outside. The general procedure for pouring is as follows:

1   Stir the glaze and blow or wipe the pot as explained.

2   Glaze the inside of the vessel first. This is done by pouring glaze inside the pot, quickly filling it up to the rim and inverting smartly (over the bucket). For large pots or bowls, a quantity of glaze is poured into the bottom of the vessel. It is then allowed to run out while the pot is held inverted at an angle of 45 degrees and rotated constantly.

■ Fig. 71. Removing the jug from the glaze.

Fig. 73. Glaze pouring.

3   Using a sponge, remove the glaze from the rim and any dribbles which have gone on the outside of the pot.

4   When the glaze on the inside is dry, the pot can be inverted on the hand (if a bowl shape), held over the glaze container and rotated while the glaze is being poured over it (see Fig. 73). For cylindrical and large pots, a thick piece of wire bent into a 'U' shape should be placed across a bowl which in turn is balanced on a whirler. The pot is then inverted to rest on the wire. Alternatively, thin strips of wood, preferably triangular in section, placed parallel across the glaze container, can be used if it is felt that the wire is unsafe. Also, make sure that the glaze container has a larger diameter than the pot to be glazed otherwise things can become very messy. The glaze is then simply poured over the pot from one point while the whirler is slowly rotated.

5   When the glaze is firm (i.e. lost its wet look), the pot can be carefully turned over and the marks on the rim

touched up. If the glaze is very untidy on the rim it can be removed with a kidney scraper and the rim lightly wiped with a sponge. The pot can be inverted again and the rim just dipped into the glaze. The pot can then be placed aside to await further decoration or firing.

One characteristic of a poured glaze is the dribble marks down the side of the pot where one thickness of glaze overlaps another. This can be a very decorative feature giving varied colour but should not be overdone, otherwise the form of the pot may be destroyed. Also, the glaze might become too thick.

Don't dither when glazing! All glazing should be done smartly with definite movements, otherwise the coating may be untidy and more often than not, too thick. If this happens the glaze should be washed off, the pot dried (on a radiator or kiln top) and a fresh attempt made.

## Spraying

This is another method of applying glaze to a pot but not one often used by the studio craftsman for a number of reasons.

The equipment needed is expensive and would include a spray gun, air compressor, spraying booth and air extractor unit. This mechanical method finds a place in industry but is not really the artist's tool.

## Cleaning up

Any rubbing down of untidy surfaces, blobs, etc., can be done when the glaze has dried out.

Pots for stoneware firing should have the glaze removed from either the footring or all of the underneath. As the fired stoneware will be vitreous and therefore waterproof, there is no necessity for glaze on the underneath. This makes kiln packing much easier as will be seen later. Earthenware pots should, of course, be left glazed. Glaze can be prevented from adhering to the underneath of a pot by brushing on molten wax or wax emulsion, prior to glazing. The wax will burn away in the firing.

# Decoration with glazes and pigments

Once the methods of glaze application are understood these can be put to a variety of decorative as well as practical uses.

## Double glazing

This technique may need a bit of practice before it is successfully mastered. It involves the use of two different coloured glazes, dipping or pouring one entirely or partially over the other. Glazes are used in this way to give a more varied surface texture or a contrast between one glaze and another. The wax or latex resist method (see Chapter 4) can be used on glazes as well as clays. The wax decoration is painted on to the applied glaze when it is firm but still damp. A second glaze is then applied. The wax repels this glaze on the decorated areas and after firing these show up as the first glaze. The wax, of course, burns away.

Double glazing using the same glaze can give subtle variations of colour.

The main points to be aware of when double glazing are:

- The glazes should be of a fairly thin consistency, otherwise the thickness of the glaze coating might be too much, causing faults after firing.
- The second glaze should be applied when the first glaze has become firm but is still damp. If the first glaze has dried out an application of a second glaze may cause it to bubble and flake off the pot. The glazes would then have to be washed off, the pot dried and a fresh start made.

## Contrast glazing

When a different glaze is wanted on the outside of the pot to the one on the inside, for contrast of colour, surface, etc., the technique is as follows:

1 Glaze the inside first by pouring (see page 86). Any dribbles on the outside of the pot can then be removed.
2 The outside glaze can then be applied either by pouring or by dipping. The dipping must be done with the pot vertically inverted. When commencing the dip, the pot must be immersed slowly to prevent the glaze splashing up the inside. The pot must also be kept perfectly vertical throughout the dip so that air, trapped on the inside, cannot escape. It is this trapped air which prevents the glaze from going up the inside of the pot.

Sometimes I use a contrast of three glazes; one on the inside (perhaps a glaze suitable as a food surface), one dipped part of the way down the outside and then, when firm, a third glaze dipped on the remaining unglazed surface. On stoneware pots the lower section of the outside may be left completely unglazed. Stoneware is waterproof and the contrasting texture of the unglazed surface is often very attractive.

## Painting with one glaze on to another

This technique is virtually self-explanatory. The pot is first of all glazed using one of the described methods and the glaze allowed to dry to the firm but damp state. A free brush decoration can then be applied using a second contrasting glaze. This is really the reverse of wax resist.

## Painting with oxides and stains on the unfired glaze

This is more or less the same as the technique just described, the difference being that oxide painting will give a stronger contrast of decoration to background. Where the oxide is thick, a black may result, particularly when using copper oxide. The glaze should once again be smooth and slightly damp when the colours are applied. The pigments are simply mixed with water, or a little base glaze, and applied with a brush.

Tin glazed ware decorated in this manner is often called maiolica, taking its name from Majorca, Italy, where it was produced. Oxides rather than stains are used as the pigments, the main ones being copper–green, cobalt–blue, manganese–brown and iron–amber.

## On-glaze painting

This refers to colour which is applied to the fired-glaze surface in the form of enamels or lustres.

Enamels or on-glaze colours are really very low temperature glazes. These can be made in the studio but are much better purchased from the supplier. They are applied to the fired-glaze surface by mixing to a suitable painting consistency with fat oil of turpentine, thinning with pure turpentine if necessary, and then applying with a brush. The pot is then given a third firing to the low temperature of 720°–780°C which is sufficient to fuse the colours on to the glaze. Because of their low firing temperature, enamels offer a much wider range of colours than underglaze colours, but because they are fused on top of the glaze they are not so durable. The colours are permanent in normal use but mechanical washing-up techniques could remove them after a period of time. However, the manufacturer's instructions as to their use should be followed closely for the best results.

Lustre and precious metal painting, using commercial products, is virtually the same as enamel painting. The only difference is that in the place of the pigment there is an iridescent metal which is deposited on the glaze surface. Commercial lustres are combined with resinates plus an oily medium. In the firing, the carbon produced by the resinate and oil reduces the metal which is deposited on the glaze surface. This type of commercial lustre should not present any problems.

A Persian-type lustre can be obtained by applying certain metallic salts such as copper carbonate or silver sulphide to an alkaline glazed surface. The copper is mixed with red ochre (2:1) and adhered to the ware with gum arabic. Having no local reducing agent in the

mixture, the lustre is formed by a reducing atmosphere in the kiln. This can be introduced either during the last hour of the firing or during the period of cooling until the kiln darkens. Ware blackened by the reduction can be cleaned with a light abrasive.

An on-glaze lustre can be obtained by mixing about 2% of copper carbonate or silver sulphide into a low firing lead borosilicate glaze. The glaze is then applied and fired as normal but a reducing atmosphere is introduced during the cooling until the black heat stage.

■ Porcelain teapot with lustre decoration and stainless steel handle.

## Note – the release of toxic metals from pottery

Glazes and colours which are not properly designed for chemical durability can be attacked by certain acids in food and drink and the toxic metals released. There is no need for alarm as long as the materials are used as specified by the supplier, i.e. in the correct proportions and fired to the correct temperature. Lead appears to have been the main source of trouble in the past. However, none of the base glazes in this book contains raw lead and they have been tested to 5% metal release which is acceptable.

Therefore there is no danger of lead poisoning as long as the glazes are correctly prepared and fired. The fritted lead and borax glazes and stoneware glazes are quite suitable for use on food contact surfaces. However, I would not recommend the painting of oxides, enamels or lustres on any surface which is to be used for this purpose. Also the addition of certain colouring agents (such as copper to a low solubility glaze) should be questioned if the surface is going to come into contact with food or drink. I would also suggest that anyone intending to make large quantities of pottery to contain food may well be advised to have samples of their ware tested, just to be on the safe side. Ceram Research now offer this service (see Suppliers).

# Glaze faults

These are the most frustrating happenings in pottery, only revealing themselves after the ware has been fired and consequently finished. Glazes giving faults can often be corrected for subsequent firings. Also pots with glaze faults can sometimes be reglazed and successfully fired. It is nevertheless extremely annoying when time has been spent on getting the pot to the glaze stage only to have it spoilt in the firing. The need for testing a glaze before mass use and the care required in repeating the conditions of a successful test firing must therefore be obvious if unnecessary glaze faults are to be avoided.

The most common faults, with the causes and suggested remedies, are as follows, remembering that prevention is better than cure.

## Crazing

This is perhaps the most common fault although it is sometimes excused as a 'decorative' feature in the so-called crackle glazes. It is nevertheless a fault which should not happen unless specially intended.

Most solids, particularly metals, expand on heating and contract on cooling. This is known as the coefficient of thermal expansion. Glaze and pot have similar coefficients of expansion and can therefore expand and contract as one material. If, however, this is not so, and the glaze contracts more than the pot, fine cracks appear all over the glaze surface. This is known as crazing. Some glazes craze weeks after they have been taken out of the kiln. Light pinging sounds are a sure indication that crazing has begun. Other glazes may be in the process of crazing when taken from the kiln. This may be the result of opening the kiln too early (above 300°C).

The remedy for crazing is either to increase the expansion of the body or lower the expansion of the glaze. This is done, strangely enough, by slightly increasing the silica content (flint) of either glaze or clay, the reason being that silica in solid form in the clay has the reverse effect of silica in molten form in the glaze. There may be a much simpler remedy for crazing in earthenware glazes, since this is often due to underfired biscuit. Therefore at some stage of the firing cycle, either in biscuit or glaze, the pot should be subjected to a temperature of more than 1100°C. If done at the biscuit stage it may take a bit longer for the applied glaze to dry, but this is worth the elimination of crazing.

## Shivering, peeling or scaling

This is the opposite of crazing and is the result of too low an expansion of the glaze. The glaze, therefore, in contraction buckles and may eventually peel off the ware. The remedies are more or less the reverse of those for crazing. The shrinkage of the glaze must be increased. This is usually done either by the addition of high shrinkage materials in the form of an alkaline or borax frit (3–5%) or an increase of felspar.

## Crawling

Crawling is when the glaze shrivels up into blobs, leaving the areas of pot in between unglazed. The basic fault is that the glaze fails to adhere to the pot during glaze application. The reasons for this are:

- Grease or dust on the pot surface.
- The glaze coating is too thick.
- Excessive shrinkage of the glaze while drying out, resulting in fractures on the unfired glaze surface. This is often caused by the glaze being applied too thickly or drying out too quickly.

The cures are therefore more or less obvious.

## Pitting, pinholing and blistering

These are similar flaws and are mainly due to the following:

- Air or gases trapped in the glaze, which are in the process of escaping when the kiln is switched off. The holes and craters caused by the escaping gas are frozen and appear on the surface of the cooled ware. The cure in this case would be to either increase the maturing temperature or lengthen the firing cycle, which could include a soaking period at the end of the firing (see Chapter 6).
- Boiling the glaze by overfiring and then switching off the kiln while this is in progress. The resulting blisters and craters are frozen and appear on the surface of the cooled ware. In this case the cure would be to lower the firing temperature.

- Glazes containing zinc or rutile sometimes pit or pinhole. In addition to reducing their quantity in the glaze, the remedy suggested above could also be tried.

## Blebbing

This is due to trapped air pockets in the clay body which expand on firing and appear as blebs on the surface of the glazed ware. This fault, however, should not arise if the clay is properly prepared and the ware carefully made.

## Summary

The above, then, is the information necessary for producing one's own glazes. The excitement of waiting for a newly prepared glaze to come out of the kiln cannot be described but has to be experienced. However, for those just beginning pottery-making, quick results are important, and while the purchase of coloured and so-called artistic glazes is rather like a baker buying a cake mix, you can compromise, and buy a standard transparent glaze and colour it yourself.

■ Porcelain bottles with lustre decoration.

■ Thrown and turned stoneware forms based on the Planets.

# 6

# Firing

Firing is the most critical period of pottery-making for it is this heating process which changes the greenware into pot and then the applied glaze mixture into a matured glaze. Firing is critical because it literally makes or breaks a pot and faults which develop during this process are usually irreversible. Also during this period, the potter has little control over the fate of the ware. One can regulate the rate of firing, the maturing temperature and the atmosphere surrounding the pots. But as for the actual pot itself, this is left entirely to the mercy of the heat. It is therefore obvious that great care needs to be taken at each stage of pottery-making if this relatively expensive process is to be successful, ensuring that any failure is not the result of carelessness or bad craftsmanship.

While every care can be taken in making the ware and firing it, the kiln in which it is fired must also be efficient. A reliable kiln is therefore one item on which no serious student of pottery can afford to economize.

## Kilns

Primitive firings were carried out in the open, possibly by heaping the greenware into a mound, covering this with dried grass and dung and then setting this alight. The fire was then kept going by stoking it with more bundles of dried grass. This is the method still used by the women potters of Nigeria and is known as 'open firing'. Firings of this type produce soft unglazed pottery and are very wasteful in terms of heat loss. It was no doubt in an effort to conserve this heat and control it that the first kiln was invented. The exact origin of this is not known but was possibly in Mesopotamia around 4000 BC.

While kilns vary in shape and size they are all basically refractory chambers into which the pots are placed to be heated by one means or another. Originally the firing chamber was heated from underneath by burning wood or some such fuel. The firing chamber was separated from the fuel chamber by some sort of refractory platform, perforated with holes and supported by a centre pillar. A chimney or flue was built into the closed top of the kiln to develop the necessary draught for sucking up the heat through the perforated holes into the firing chamber and then out. This was the system used in Britain by the Romans, the principle of which is still used in many parts of the world today. Kilns of this type are known as up-draught open kilns. Another system in which the heat is drawn into the top of the firing chamber and out through flues in the floor is known as a down-draught open kiln.

When it was found necessary to protect the ware from the flames as is the case with some delicate pottery and some glazes, refractory containers were developed into which the ware was placed. These containers are known as saggars and are usually drum shaped.

A further development in protecting the ware from the flames was a refractory chamber built inside the firing chamber. This is known as a muffle and of course eliminates the need for saggars.

Of the combustible fuels used in firing kilns, gas has proved to be the most economical and convenient. In more recent times, however, an even more convenient 'fuel' has been adopted for heating kilns. This is the electric current. It is therefore in the range of kilns heated by either electricity or gas that the modern potter will find a suitable one.

## The electric kiln

This type of kiln differs from all the others because its heat is not developed from combustion but from an electric current passing through elements. These elements are set into grooves which are cut into the firing chamber walls, floor and sometimes door. The current passes through the elements and the firing rate is simply controlled by either a rotary switch with settings at low, medium and high, an energy regulator calibrated from 0 to 100 or a microprocessor controller which has been programmed to replace the manual control of firing. For a slow temperature rise,

using an energy regulator, the setting should be around 40; the higher the setting, the more rapid the temperature rise.

The electric kiln is undoubtedly the most suitable type of kiln for studio, college or school purposes for the following reasons:

- It obviously requires no flue, although an extractor fan is advisable.
- It can therefore be sited on any floor level depending on its size and weight.
- It is clean, compact and so well insulated that fire risk is virtually eliminated.
- It gives an even temperature.
- It is easy to fire and little experience is necessary to operate it quite successfully.
- Under normal firing conditions it will require little maintenance. This usually amounts to the replacement of elements from time to time or occasionally repairing damaged brickwork. Instructions for operation and maintenance are usually included in the sale of a new kiln and therefore need little explanation here. For the repair of older kilns advice can be obtained from the respective manufacturer along with the necessary materials (replacement elements, refractory bricks and refractory cement). For complex repairs the manufacturer will usually give a quotation for undertaking the work as long as descriptive and specific information can be supplied.

## Reduction in a electric kiln

While regular high firing can shorten the life of elements, the greatest wear occurs if the kiln is used for reduction firings. This is because the protective oxide layer, which forms on the elements in oxidizing conditions, is removed, with a resultant loss of durability (see Special firings – reductions, page 106). However electric kilns can be used for reduction, though rather expensively, so long as the following procedure is adhered to.

Periodically, or as soon as a discolouration is noticed on the elements (normal colour light grey), they should be re-oxidized by firing the kiln empty with the spy hole open and damper partially open to a temperature of 100°C below maximum for a period of seven to eight hours.

There is now an electric kiln available which has been specifically designed for reduction and high temperature firings. This is fired with silicon carbide rod elements whereas other kilns are fitted with nichrome (nickel and chrome) or kanthal elements. This new type of element will undoubtedly be developed further and more generally used, but until it is, the above advice is the general procedure for reduction using standard elements.

## Purchasing an electric kiln

There is at present such a wide choice of kilns on the market that selecting the right one is often difficult. The following considerations are therefore offered as guidance for making a selection:

- Funds available.
- Type and amount of work to be fired.
- Maximum firing temperature. Kilns firing to 1300°C offer more scope and are therefore the best buy in the long term.
- Siting – amount of room available. This will include access to the site, although some kilns can be assembled on site. Make sure that the floor will support the weight of the kiln and load.
- Electricity supply – while there are some small kilns which will run off a normal 13/15 amp domestic supply without the need for any special wiring, most useful kilns require connecting to either a single-phase or three-phase mains supply. The type of supply must be stated when ordering a kiln. Information on type and rating can be obtained from the local Electricity Board.
- Running costs.
- Delivery – make sure that the conditions of delivery are studied and that the supplier will

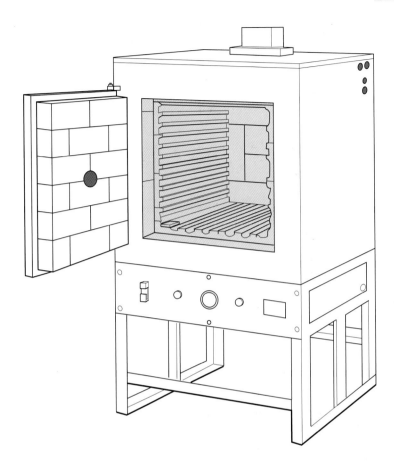

- Fig. 74. An electric kiln.

undertake delivery and siting of the kiln. Some suppliers will only deliver and that leaves the unloading and siting the responsibility of the customer. With an average kiln weighing approximately 7 cwt (355.6 kg) this can present a serious problem.
- After sales – make sure that if you are undertaking your own maintenance, replacement parts, etc. can be obtained from the kiln supplier.

While it is impossible to suggest the size or make of kiln one should begin with, some idea is given by the following generalized dimensions.

## Small kiln–1300°C

|  | width | depth | height |
|---|---|---|---|
| firing chamber dimensions | 10 in. × 10 in. × 13 in. | | |
|  | (254 mm × 254 mm × 330 mm) | | |
| overall dimensions: | 24 in. × 27 in. × 30 in. | | |
|  | (610 mm × 686 mm × 762 mm) | | |
| nett weight: | 2¾ cwt, 140 kg | | |
| power rating: | 3.25 kW | | |
| electricity supply: | 240 V single-phase 13/15 amp | | |
|  | (possible) | | |

## Medium kiln–1300°C

|  | width | depth | height |
|---|---|---|---|
| firing chamber dimensions | 15 in. × 24 in. × 16 in. | | |
|  | (381mm × 610 mm × 406 mm) | | |
| overall dimensions: | 30 in. × 40 in. × 57 in. | | |
|  | (762 mm × 1015 mm × 1422 mm) | | |
| nett weight: | 6¾ cwt, 345 kg | | |
| power rating: | 8.0 kW | | |
| electricity supply: | 240 V single-phase – 40 amp | | |

(For an example of this type of kiln see Fig. 74.) A list of reputable suppliers is given at the back of the book.

## The gas kiln

Kilns fired by gas incorporate most of the qualities required for producing any type of pottery. They also provide the most controlled and economical form of heating where this is supplied by burning fuel rather than using electrical energy.

Gas kilns are usually of either the down-draught open or closed muffle types. The advantage of the former is the ease with which reducing conditions can be introduced. In this type of kiln, however, it is possible, if fired by an inexperienced person, to damage certain glazes. As explained, the use of saggars will prevent this happening but will obviously inhibit the kiln's reduction qualities (see Reduction firing on page 106). The muffle-type kiln would, therefore, seem to be ideal as reduction conditions can be achieved as explained in reduction firing. However, muffle kilns

have their faults in that too quick a firing can damage the muffle refractories. This results in the muffle being continually repaired or replaced altogether. I am sure that this is one of the reasons why suppliers of gas-muffle kilns are becoming increasingly difficult to find. In fact at the present time, I can find only one and the kiln obtainable from this supplier is too small to be of much use to the potter.

In comparison to electric kilns, gas kilns have many disadvantages. Some of these are as follows:

- They are heavier, although some models are now relatively 'light' due to the use of 'space age' refractories.
- They are bulkier with additional space having to be allowed for pipework. If firing on LPG (Propane), outside storage space would have to be available for fuel tanks or storage bottles.
- Provision has to be made for a flue pipe leading to a suitable outlet with enough fire insulation around the flue pipe where this may pass through floors, roof, etc. Adequate flue ventilation can be a problem in some areas because of by-laws.
- Siting, therefore, because of the above three points, is much more of a problem than for electric kilns.
- More skill and experience is required to fire them.
- Gas kilns are dearer to buy than electric kilns.

The gas kiln is, therefore, an excellent tool in the hands of a professional but is certainly not recommended for the beginner. Also its practical disadvantages, compared with the electric kiln, must now rate it in many cases the potter's second choice.

# Kiln furniture

This is the collective term for refractory items used in packing a kiln. While sets of furniture are supplied to suit specific kiln designs (at extra cost), items of furniture can be bought from specialist suppliers as well as from the kiln merchant. Make sure that when purchasing kiln furniture it has been designed to withstand the temperature to which the kiln is being fired, and also that the bats are of a size which allows approximately a half-inch (12.70 mm) space between bat and kiln wall. This permits good circulation of heat.

The items which make up kiln furniture are as follows:

- Bats or shelves – refractory slabs on which the pots are placed.
- Props and prop extensions – used for spacing and supporting the bats. These are available in a range of heights and come in two systems; the tubular and the castellated interlocking.
- Pin cranks – a tiered system for supporting tiles and small plates.
- Tile cranks – a more robust system for supporting tiles in tier formation.
- Stilts, spurs, saddles – used for supporting mainly earthenware-glazed pots to prevent them from sticking to the bats. Stoneware pots usually have the glaze removed from their bases prior to firing and therefore these supports are not needed. Stilts are used for supporting regular-shaped pots while spurs and saddles can be arranged to cope with irregular ones.
- Nichrome wire – in addition to certain gauges of this refractory wire being used for making kiln elements, a fine gauge can be used for stringing or supporting beads during firing. (For illustrations of kiln furniture see Fig. 75.)

# Temperature indicators and controllers

While many experienced potters pride themselves on being able to tell the approximate temperature of a kiln by observing, through a spy hole, the colour of the firing chamber, this is of no use to the student. The two main forms of accurate temperature indicators are at present the pyrometer and the pyrometric cone. These two aids should be used jointly as their purposes are slightly different.

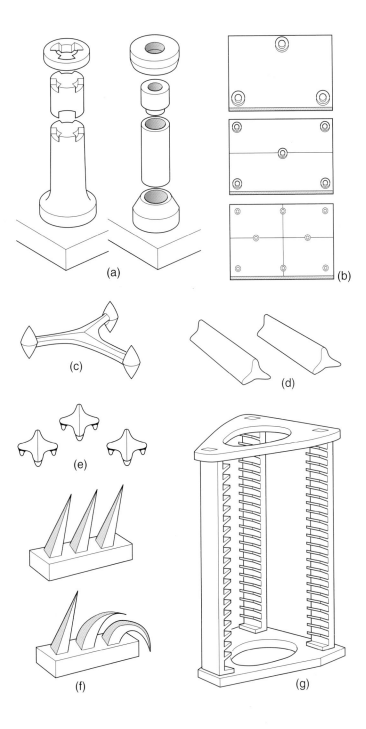

■ Fig. 75. Kiln furniture. (a) Props – castellated and tubular; (b) Bats, showing propping systems; (c) Stilt; (d) Saddles; (e) Pyrometric cones; (f) Tile crank.

## The pyrometer

This is a temperature-indicating dial which is mounted on to the outside of the kiln or a nearby wall to give readings of the kiln temperature, transmitted by a thermocouple inside the kiln. The dial is usually calibrated 0–1300°C. The pyrometer is a very useful instrument as it indicates the rate at which the firing is proceeding, thus allowing the firing to be speeded up or slowed down if necessary. Therefore, of the many available kiln accessories, the pyrometer is one item which must really be regarded as standard equipment. Of the other accessories, designed to give a more automatic firing, it is up to the individual to decide which equipment is relevant to his need. For those interested in automation, either by desire or necessity, full details can be found in the suppliers' catalogues and instruction leaflets.

## Pyrometric cones

These are small pyramids of compressed glaze materials which bend over at certain temperatures when supported vertically in the kiln. The cones are generally used in a stick of three. These are arranged in the order of one to bend over just below the required temperature, a second to bend over on the required temperature and a third to be used as a guard cone against overfiring (see Fig. 75). The cones can be set in a manufactured refractory socket or sunk to a depth of ¼ in. (6.350 mm) into flat slabs of grogged stoneware clay. The space between the cones should be approximately ⅛ in. (3.175 mm). They should be set with a slight tilt so that they bend in the desired direction making sure that this will not be on to the ware.

Cones may give a false reading if they are badly set (tilted at the wrong angle). When setting the cones in clay, holes can be made with a matchstick in the clay surface to allow the moisture to escape, thus reducing the risk of the clay shattering on heating. A safer way is to allow the clay to dry first but this is often inconvenient. I often set cones in grogged clay pressed into old castellated prop supports. By this method I can adjust the cones to the exact height of the spy-hole, if a kiln shelf is at an inconvenient level. Make sure that the cones are clearly visible through the spy-hole in the door. This can easily be checked by placing a lighted match, supported in a bit of clay with the sited cones. They should then be clearly visible through the spy-hole. Cones may also be placed elsewhere in the kiln, not to be seen, but to check after firing whether or not the temperature has been even throughout the kiln.

The pyrometric cone has changed little since it was first introduced in 1886 by the German chemist Dr Hermann Seger (cones often being called 'Seger cones'). In addition to the German Seger cone there is the English Staffordshire cone and the American Orton cone. The difference between the three is that their number-temperature designation varies. This is because they are calibrated to collapse according to different rates of temperature rise. For example, a Seger cone marked 1a will collapse at 1125°C so long as the temperature rises at a rate of 150°C per hour. A Staffordshire cone marked 1 will collapse at 1100°C so long as the temperature rises at a rate of 240°C per hour. If one fires at a rate slower than the rate for which the cones being used are calculated, the temperature at which they collapse will be lower than that indicated or vice versa. This is because the maturing of pottery and glazes is a time-temperature process rather than temperature alone. In other words, because a kiln is at a temperature of 1100°C it does not follow that a glaze (or cone) will be fully matured if the time necessary for the heat to work upon the glaze (or cone) is too short. From this it can be seen why the use of cones is so important as an additional indication of temperature to the pyrometer. While the latter will gauge temperature rise and the actual temperature of the kiln, the cones will show the effect of the temperature or heat-work done. This is most important in glaze firings for while the pyrometer will indicate temperature the cone will indicate the state of the glaze.

| Cone no. | Bending °C | Temperature °F | Colour in kiln | Temperature required for |
|---|---|---|---|---|
| 022 | 600 | 1112 | Colour begins | |
| 021 | 650 | 1202 | to show | |
| 020 | 670 | 1238 | | |
| 019 | 690 | 1274 | | |
| 018 | 710 | 1310 | Dull red | |
| 017 | 730 | 1346 | | On glaze enamels, |
| 016 | 750 | 1382 | | lustres. Soft raku |
| 015 | 790 | 1454 | | |
| 014 | 815 | 1499 | Red and cherry | Harder raku |
| 013 | 835 | 1535 | | |
| 012 | 855 | 1571 | | |
| 011 | 880 | 1616 | | |
| 010 | 900 | 1652 | | |
| 09 | 920 | 1688 | | |
| 08 | 940 | 1724 | | |
| 07 | 960 | 1760 | | |
| 06 | 980 | 1796 | Dull to light | |
| 05 | 1000 | 1832 | cherry | |
| 04 | 1020 | 1868 | | |
| 03 | 1040 | 1904 | | |
| 02 | 1060 | 1940 | | |
| 01 | 1080 | 1976 | | Biscuit. |
| 1 | 1100 | 2012 | | Earthenware |
| 2 | 1120 | 2048 | Dark to pale | glaze |
| 3 | 1140 | 2084 | orange | |
| 4 | 1160 | 2120 | | |
| 5 | 1180 | 2156 | | |
| 6 | 1200 | 2192 | | |
| 7 | 1230 | 2246 | | |
| 8 | 1250 | 2282 | Yellowish | Stoneware glaze |
| 9 | 1280 | 2336 | white to white | |
| 10 | 1300 | 2372 | | Porcelain glaze |

To convert °C to °F the equation is: $(\frac{9}{5}°C + 32)$

To convert °F to °C the equation is: $\frac{5}{9}(°F - 32)$

This may all sound rather complex to the beginner, but it is really quite straightforward. Just remember to check (from the suppliers' catalogues) the number stamped on the cone with the recommended collapsing temperature against the calibrated rate of firing. If, for any reason, the rate of firing is not the same as the one for which the cone has been calibrated, then simply keep a record of the firing cycle in the kiln log-book and note the behaviour of the cone at the supposed maturing temperature. If it collapses at a lower or a higher temperature than the one stated, it will always do so as long as the firing cycle follows the same pattern.

In an effort to co-ordinate temperature observation and the type of ware made at the different temperatures, I have compiled the chart (left). The cone numbers used are for Staffordshire cones calibrated on the 240°C per hour rate of firing. It can be seen from the chart that cone 1 represents 1100°C. Consecutive numbers with '0' in front decrease in temperature from 1100°C at an approximate rate of 20°C.

Consecutive numbers without an '0' in front increase in temperature from 1100°C by the same amount.

There are more cones than given in the chart for intermediate and higher temperatures. However, the ones needed to fire the pottery and glazes described in this book are all included.

# Biscuit firing

While some pottery, for example, salt-glazed stoneware, is fired from the greenware to the finished glazed stage in one go, the general practice is to fire the ware twice. The first firing, when the greenware is changed into pot, is called the biscuit firing and pottery at this stage of completion is referred to as 'biscuit'.

## Packing for biscuit

Packing a 'biscuit' kiln is relatively straightforward. The aim is to get as much ware as possible into the kiln without packing the pots so tightly together that the heat cannot fully circulate, or the pots expand freely. When the greenware is thoroughly dry, any unpleasant sharp edges or bits of unwanted clay can be removed with wire wool. The ware can then be packed into the kiln in the following way:

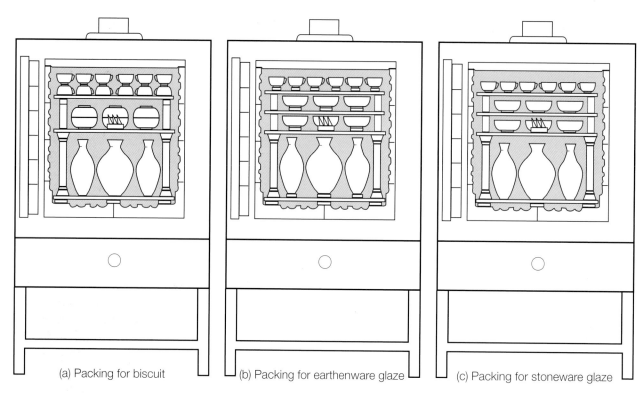

(a) Packing for biscuit  (b) Packing for earthenware glaze  (c) Packing for stoneware glaze

■ Fig. 76. Packing a kiln.

■ Bowls, plates and dishes can be stacked one inside the other, footring to inside base, with the largest and strongest ware at the bottom. A sprinkling of sand or some such refractory material should separate the ware to allow the pots to expand and contract freely. Be very careful when placing pots one inside the other, particularly bowls with inturned lips, or they may be inseparable after firing due to different rates of shrinkage. Ware of the same size may be placed rim to rim or foot to foot (Fig. 76(a)). The maximum number of pieces to stack depends on their strength and, of course, the potter's experience in packing and firing. Do not be tempted into false economy by over-stacking. A little wasted space is worth much less than a broken pot.

Among other things it is worth a trip around an industrial pottery to see the kiln packers loading up the trucks to go into the big tunnel kilns. The ware is packed on to the trucks so skilfully one would think that the truck and ware had been cast from one big mould.

■ Ware with handles may also be stacked if the shapes allow it, for example, cups rim to rim. Care should be taken to keep the handles away from the hot parts of the kiln (the elements in electric kilns), otherwise they may warp. Turn them towards the centre of the kiln (Fig. 76(a)). Spouts can also suffer if the same care is not taken.

■ Lidded ware should be fired with the lids in place. If the lid fits comfortably in the dry greenware state, it should fit after firing. If the lid is not fired in the pot it should be fired as near to it as possible, otherwise an uneven firing would give different shrinkages. This would then result in a misfit after firing. Flat lids with raised knobs can be placed inverted in the pot to allow stacking.

- Large tiles for wall panels, etc. should be placed on a carpet of sand which has been sieved on to the kiln shelf prior to packing. This will allow free expansion and contraction. Remember that when packing there must be room for free expansion of all wares and that ware stacked too high or too close together may be false economy in terms of cracking, warping and uneven firing. Only one pot at the bottom of the stack has to give way to cause possible damage to the others.

- Make sure that an inconspicuous hole is made in any ware which has a pocket of enclosed air, for example hollowed out animal models. This is so that on heating, the expanding air can escape. Forgetting to do this could result in a damaged model.

- Ware decorated with underglaze colours or oxides should not be stacked as the colours could volatilize on to other ware or even cause the ware to stick together.

## Arrangement of kiln bats

While is is possible to stack a biscuit kiln, particularly a small one, without using bats, the risks as explained above must be considered. It is, therefore, usual to make up shelves using one or more bats at different levels in the kiln. Some kilns take one bat per shelf, some take two or more. However many bats are required, they are supported on one of the propping systems (see Kiln furniture) which are set in a triangular arrangement (see Fig. 75 (b)). This is a stronger method of support than by placing props at four corners of the bat.

Before the first layer of pots is set, the props to support the first shelf (the second if the floor shelf is counted), should be arranged as described. The height of the props should be no less than ¼ in. (6.350 mm) above the level of the tallest ware. This is to ensure a sufficient gap between the ware and the above shelf to allow for the circulation of heat and for expansion. The first layer of pots is then set and any necessary adjustment made to the level of the props. The bats for the next shelf are then put into place.

It is a good idea, after placing a bat, to lift it just off each prop in turn to allow the props to settle back freely into position. The props are then arranged as before for the next shelf. Make sure that the second set of props is directly above the first, otherwise the shelf might crack in firing (see Fig. 76). The packing can then continue in this manner until completed.

When arranging bats it is not always necessary to make up a full shelf. For example, the back of the kiln may be packed with small pots using bats, while the front is used for single standing large shapes. But no matter how the kiln is packed, remember to leave room for the cones. Note:

- Before using any kiln furniture it should be thoroughly inspected for damage. Faulty kiln furniture can ruin many pots in firing. A bat can be tested for cracks by supporting it at its centre on the hand and tapping it sharply with a knuckle. If it rings, it is all right, while a dull or buzzing sound means trouble and the bat should not be used.

- It is better to give new kiln furniture a drying-out firing before it is used to support pots.

- When not in use, kiln furniture should be stacked tidily in a dry place with the bats stacked on their edges. This can save a lot of unnecessary damage.

- When propping, a single unit is much stronger than a lot of smaller units. A base or pad used at the top and bottom of the prop will distribute the load more evenly on the bats and should always be used when a prop bridges two or more bats.

- When packing, distribute the load of the pots as evenly as possible over the surface of the bat.

## Firing procedure

When the packing is completed (with the cones set), the door is closed and the spy-hole and damper opened. The firing should then be carried out as slowly and evenly as possible. The procedure is as follows:

1   Switch on the kiln to heat up very slowly (preferably overnight). On electric kilns this means turning to low, energy regulator to 30 or engaging the microprocessor controller. On a gas kiln the burners would be turned on low. The speed with which a kiln heats up will, of course, depend on its size and type relative to the heat input. However, the aim particularly at this early stage of firing, is for a slow as well as even build-up of heat. The first stage is to remove the water or plasticity and is known as the 'smoking' or 'steaming' stage. If this is done too quickly expanding moisture, changing into steam, may shatter the ware, particularly thick pieces. At 150°C the smoking stage should be complete.

2   If the firing is done overnight, this stage should be safely passed by the morning and the kiln can be turned up slightly. Settings for heat input will have to be worked out by experience with a particular kiln. However, the firing should proceed slowly, say at a temperature rise of 50°C per hour, through the next stages which are:

– at approximately 283°C, when the silica crystals ($\alpha$ cristobalite) in the clay change to $\beta$ cristobalite. While $\beta$ cristobalite has the same chemical composition as $\alpha$ cristobalite, it has a slightly larger volume.

– at approximately 573°C, when the silica crystals ($\alpha$ quartz) in the clay change to $\beta$ quartz. Again the $\beta$ crystal has the same chemical composition as the $\alpha$ crystal but has a larger volume. This is an important change in the silica crystals and is known as quartz inversion. If the firing is rushed when these silica modifications are taking place, the sudden volume changes cause strains in the body, which result in the ware cracking. This fault in fired ware is known as dunting and is usually brought about if the kiln cools too rapidly when the $\beta$ silica crystals are changing back to $\alpha$ crystals.

– from 450°–700°C, when the chemically combined water is driven off, changing the clay irreversibly into pot. During this stage more steam is given off and, if hurried, shattering may occur for the reasons already given.

3   When the temperature is at 700°C the inside of the kiln will be showing a dull red colour. The spy-hole can be closed and on electric kilns the ventilation damper replaced. The heat controls can be turned up and the firing continued at a fairly slow and even pace. A temperature rise of approximately 100°C per hour should be aimed for. This, of course, can be controlled by adjusting the heat controls in accordance with the reading on the pyrometer.

4   At 900°C the organic matter along with the sulphur compounds and carbon will have been driven off. Therefore, all biscuit (with the exception of raku ware) should be taken above 900°C, for if these impurities remain to be burnt out during a higher glaze firing, they will cause blemishes on the glaze surface.

5   As the temperature rises, the pot will start to vitrify, becoming less and less porous as the particles fuse and shrink into a hard dense mass. It is at this point, before complete vitrification takes place, that the biscuit firing is terminated. It is difficult to give an average temperature for terminating a biscuit firing, as different clays vitrify at different temperatures. For example, many red clays with a high iron context (flux) will vitrify around 1060°C, while buff (grey) clays may not vitrify until 1200°C +. However, unless separate firings for the different clays are possible (this being the best solution), I would suggest that all biscuit should be taken to 1100°C.

6   When the pyrometer and the centre cone indicate that the required temperature has been reached, the firing can be terminated by simply switching off the heat. All dampers and spy-holes should be closed so that the kiln can cool down as slowly as possible. Quick cooling can cause similar damage to quick heating. Therefore the kiln should be left to cool down in the same time as it took to fire it. When cool (below 200°C) the kiln can be opened and unpacked.

# Glaze firing

## Preparing the kiln furniture

If one has access to two kilns it is good practice to keep the first one for biscuit firing and the second for glaze or glost firing. However, as this luxury is usually confined to educational establishments and most of us have to manage with one kiln, the following preparations should be made before packing for a glaze firing.

1   Carefully brush out the kiln to remove any bits of pot or loose refractory lining which may fall on to the glazed ware and ruin it.

2   A coat of bat wash should be applied to the upper surface of any bats intended for use. The wash can be purchased as bat wash or made of some refractory material (china clay and flint in equal parts), mixed with water to a thick creamy consistency. Alternatively a thin layer of fine sand can be shaken on to the bat from a sieve. The practice of dusting the bats with dry powered flint is not recommended because of the danger of silicosis through inhaling the virtually invisible silica dust. Lining the bats protects them from blobs of glaze which might drop off the pot in the firing. Also it will prevent the unglazed bases of stoneware pots, on vitrification, from temporarily sticking to the bats. If this happens, bits of pot tend to splinter from the base due to the ware being unable to expand and contract freely. A ½ in. (12.70 mm) border of lining should be removed from the edge of the bat by either wiping or brushing to prevent any dropping on the pots below when the bat is placed. If previous linings have become untidy these should be removed and fresh ones applied. Persistent blobs of glaze can be carefully chipped away with a hammer and old chisel.

3   Check that all furniture is in good condition. Also make sure that if the firing is to stoneware temperatures (1300°C), the kiln furniture is designed to withstand that heat. If one purchases only high temperature furniture it will save much confusion and can, of course, be used for the dual purpose of low and high temperature firings.

## Packing for an earthenware glaze firing

Make sure that the pots to be fired are at hand and that all the applied glaze is dry. If pots of similar height have been put together it will make the packing much easier. Pots for an earthenware glaze firing should be glazed all over if they are to be completely waterproof.

To prevent the glazed underneath of the ware from sticking to the shelf bats in the firing, the pots are placed on the various types of supports listed under kiln furniture. However, care must be taken when selecting a support to ensure that it is of the correct size and strength to support the pot firmly under the strains of the firing. If using stilts, make sure that there is a least ¼ in. (6.350 mm) clearance between the stilt cross-piece and the pot base. This will prevent the pot and stilt being welded together if the glaze is slightly runny in the molten state.

It is very difficult to stock stilts that will fit every size of footring or pot base and this can be a source of frustration and annoyance when packing. Spurs are therefore perhaps the best means of support as using them avoids this problem. They can be arranged to give very firm support for more or less any shape and size of pot without the danger from running glaze.

While stilts and spurs support the ware in fine points, the glaze around these points should be as thin as possible. If the glaze is thick, a large piece of stilt point will remain embedded in the glaze when the rest of the stilt drops or is tapped off after firing. This will have to be carefully removed on a grindstone. In fact glaze may be virtually removed from footrings leaving just the finest film to prevent water absorption. Water (from washing dishes, etc.) absorbed into unglazed porous pots will leave a damp mark if placed on a polished wood surface and this can prove more than difficult to remove! The underneath of tiles are usually scraped and sponged free of glaze and then can stand on the tile cranks.

Unlike biscuit packing, pots packed for a glaze firing should be amply spaced leaving approximately ¼ in. (6.350 mm) between each one, otherwise they might come from the kiln stuck together. Remember to leave the same space between the shelf above and the kiln walls and roof. Placing the pots too near the elements in an electric kiln can cause local over-firing. This, however, is unlikely to happen because the edge of the shelf will be approximately ½ in. (12.70 mm) from the elements.

When placing the dry glazed ware, be careful not to smudge decoration or to handle pots with fingers covered in pigment from decoration. Hands should be inspected after placing each piece, and if dirty should be sponged clean. Also care must be taken not to knock bits of glaze off the pots by mishandling or catching them on the kiln shelves, etc. If this happens the damaged areas must be touched up with glaze applied with a brush. Glazes for this purpose should be kept close by and well stirred. When dry, the repaired patches can be rubbed down with the finger.

When the kiln is packed (Fig 76(b)), the appropriate cones can be set and the firing can begin.

## Packing for a stoneware firing

This process is much the same as for earthenware. However, the pots will not require stilting, etc. because, as already explained, the underneaths will be free of glaze. The shelves and props should, of course, be sound and of high temperature strength. Great care should be taken to ensure that the props are in alignment for the strains and stresses in stoneware are greater than in earthenware. Bats should be well lined as explained. The main reason for this is not to protect them from spots of glaze, as in earthenware, for stoneware glazes are not that fluid, but to allow for free expansion and contraction of the pot.

Finally, a quick inspection should be made of the underside of the bat before it is placed, just to make sure that this is free from bits which could drop on to and damage the pots below.

When the kiln is packed the cones can then be set and the kiln is ready to fire (Fig. 76(c)).

## Glaze firing procedure

Fewer problems arise in the glaze firing than in the biscuit firing because the pot has already undergone its chemical change. However, too quick a firing and cooling can result in glaze faults and also pot faults due to the changing silica crystals. A steady firing, therefore, may be more economical in the long run. The procedure would then be similar to biscuit firing and is as follows:

1  Switch on the kiln to a low heat (again preferably overnight). By the morning the kiln should have slowly reached 600°C. At this temperature the glaze will have undergone its initial shrinkage; organic matter such as wax and mineral carbonates will have been released and chemically combined water in any clay content in the glaze will have been driven off. The spy-hole and ventilator damper should, therefore, be left for all vapours to escape.

2  At 700°C, when the kiln shows dull red, the spy-hole and ventilator damper can be closed and the controls operated to give a temperature rise which can be as quick as good final results permit.

3  As the maturing temperature of the glaze is approached (indicated by the pyrometer and the collapse of the first of the three cones) the firing can be slowed down in the preparation for a 'soaking' period. The soaking period is a length of time in which the kiln is maintained at a constant temperature, this being the maturing temperature of the glaze. The purpose of a 'soak' is to allow the temperature to become uniform throughout the kiln, allowing any gases trapped under the glaze surface to escape, and to allow the glaze to mature properly and even out. (A soaking period can also round off the biscuit firing so as to allow the heat time to fully penetrate the pot, particularly when thick ware is being fired.) The soaking time usually lasts from three-quarters of an hour to two hours, depending on the type of ware and glaze being fired.

   Various methods are used to maintain the temperature depending on the type of kiln and controls being used. On an electric kiln fitted with a rotary control switch, the medium setting would be adopted. If an energy regulator is fitted, the setting would be 50–60 on the scale. A microprocessor controller would be programmed to accommodate this. The spy-hole may be left open to help control the temperature and also to clear the atmosphere in the kiln. On a gas kiln, the temperature would be maintained by adjusting burners and damper. While accurate temperature control is mainly a question of experience at firing a particular kiln, the need for a pyrometer is obvious at this stage of the firing procedure.

4    At the end of the soaking period the kiln can be switched off and spy-holes and dampers shut. The kiln should then be allowed to cool in its own time (approximately the same time as it took to fire). The temperature should be below 200°C before any attempt is made to unpack the kiln (however tempting). Leaving the kiln alone until it is quite cool is the best policy.

Note: As already stated, bits of stilts can remain attached to earthenware pots even when the main stilt has been removed. These are often razor sharp and can cut fingers quite badly if care is not taken in unpacking the kiln. Remove these sharp points on a grindstone as soon as possible.

# Firing cycle

It is impossible to suggest a firing cycle without knowing the type and size of kiln being used. However, an average time of 10 hours is usually given for firings of up to 1100°C and 14 hours for firings of up to 1300°C. This is not particularly informative for beginners confronted with firing their own kiln. Specific information about the capabilities of a particular kiln (how quickly it will reach maximum temperature, etc.) should be obtained from the respective supplier. Nevertheless it may be of some use if I give a time plan (as a guide only) which I have found suitable for electric kilns of similar dimensions to the ones given for a medium kiln (see Electric kiln) with power ratings of between 6.0 and 8.0 kW.

The time plan is as follows:

- Rotary switch 'Low'       (overnight if possible)
  Energy regulator 30      (spy-hole and ventilator damper open)

(A time switch can be fitted to the power supply so that the kiln can be set to come on during the night. Otherwise approximately 10 hours should be allowed on this setting for the temperature to have reached 500°C by 9 a.m. the following morning. No matter how long the kiln setting is on 'Low' the temperature will not rise much above 600°C.)

- *9 a.m.* – rotary switch 'Med'  – temperature 500°C
  energy regulator 70        (spy-hole and damper open)
- *11 a.m.* – rotary switch 'High' – temperature 700°C
  energy regulator 100       (spy-hole and damper shut)
- *1–2 p.m.*                – temperature 1100°C
  Biscuit and earthenware glost temperature reached.

(A soaking period can then be introduced by opening the spy-hole and turning the switch to 'Med' to 50–60. After this the kiln can be switched off and the spy-hole shut. If stoneware temperatures are required the firing can simply carry on.)

- Electric kiln.

■ *4 p.m.*      – temperature 1250°C
Medium stoneware temperature reached.

(A soaking period can be introduced and then the kiln switched off as explained.) A microprocessor controlled kiln can be programmed to follow the above cycle or any firing cycle depending on the capabilities of the kiln.

This firing cycle is longer than the averages given, but I find it economical in terms of long element life and elimination of pot damage. However, this cycle can be quickened, particularly for stoneware, by using the 'medium' instead of the 'low' setting for the initial stages of firing. This would mean 700°C would be reached in 8–9 hours. A turn up to 'high' at 9 a.m. would mean that 1250°C would be reached by 2 p.m. I have fired my microprocessor controlled kiln to 1125°C in 6¾ hours at a rate of 150°C for the first 3 hours and 200°C for the rest with a 10 minute soak. The new programmers can be fitted to old manually controlled kilns (provided they have a contactor) using a socket conversion kit.

# Special firings

In addition to the basic biscuit- and glaze-firing procedures there are other types of firing which differ in temperature and atmosphere as well as procedure. These are as follows:

## Reduction firing

When the carbon of a fuel combines with oxygen from the air in the presence of heat, combustion or burning takes place. If the air (oxygen) supply is cut off, then the carbon (seen as black smoke), in an effort to complete combustion, will try to find oxygen from elsewhere. If the oxygen supply (air) is removed or cut off from the kiln atmosphere then the carbon of the fuel will use the oxygen from the metal oxides in the clay and glazes thus reducing them to what is known as a lower oxide. This brings about the change in colour explained in Chapter 5.

A reducing atmosphere is easy to achieve in an open kiln (one in which the burning fuel passes into the firing chamber) by simply restricting the air supply to the burning fuel. In open gas kilns this is done by manipulation of air valves and dampers. In muffle kilns and electric kilns where the firing chamber atmosphere is always oxidizing and clear, carbonaceous fuel has to be introduced (through the spy-hole). The oxygen in the chamber will soon be used up and then the smoky carbon will combine with the oxygen in the body and glaze to complete its combustion.

Fuels used for reducing this type of kiln are usually in the form of wood chips or moth balls which are introduced into the firing chamber through an iron tube inserted into the spy-hole. The tube is then quickly removed and the spy-hole shut to prevent the fumes from escaping.

As a reducing atmosphere is generally used at stoneware temperatures, the reduction can be started at around 1100°C and maintained up to the maturing temperature of the glaze. A short oxidizing period is advisable at the end of the firing to clear the kiln atmosphere.

I have had many successful reduction firings in a medium-size gas-muffle kiln using moth balls. These are introduced as explained at the rate of ten balls every 20 minutes from 1100°–1250°C. The door of the kiln, prior to reduction, is sealed around the edge with grogged clay to prevent the smoke (free carbon) from escaping. However, some does escape and there should be good ventilation in the room when reducing in a closed muffle because there is always a certain amount of carbon dioxide and even carbon monoxide fumes around the kiln. When reducing with solid fuel (moth balls) the immediate area around the fuel entry should be kept clear of ware as this may suffer damage from the spontaneous ignition.

Reduction in an electric kiln can be achieved in the same ways as in a muffle kiln but, as already explained, the consumption of oxygen includes the protective oxide coating on the kanthal elements (see Reduction in an electric kiln). However the new silicon carbide rod element seems to be the answer to this problem, but is at the moment more expensive than the kanthal element.

## Raku firing

This low temperature firing should not present many problems and can be carried out quickly in most small electric and muffle-type kilns. I have done raku firings in both of these types of kiln which on reaching the required temperature (approximately 860°C for the glaze listed) took about 20 minutes to melt the glaze. This would have been quicker but for the fact that heat was lost when the doors were opened and had to be built up again.

The pots are given a low biscuit firing (800°C) and glazed in the normal way. The procedure is then as follows:

1   Heat the kiln to the required temperature, indicated by cone or colour.
2   Assemble the pots, close at hand, having already applied the glaze and colour. Make sure that this is quite dry by

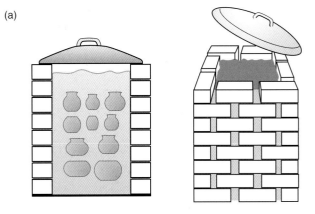

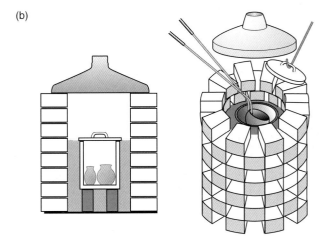

■ Fig. 77. Home-built kilns. (a) Kiln for sawdust firing; (b) Kiln for raku firing.

standing the pots around the top of the kiln and that the glaze has been well removed from the footrings of the pots.
3   Carefully and slowly open the kiln door standing well back and with the hands protected in fireproof gloves.
4   Place the pots quickly in the kiln using the long 3 ft. (0.9144 m) tongs. Close the door.
5   Observe the state of the glaze through the spy-hole. When really shiny, open the kiln and remove the pots with the tongs. Then either:

■ Raku forms.

– place the pot on a fire-brick to cool, or;
– plunge the pot into a metal bucket of water to cool instantly. If the pot has been made of the correct grogged clay, the glaze will craze but the pot will not shatter (low expansion and shrinkage), or;
– plunge the pot into a metal bowl or bucket of fine wood shavings for a minute or two and then into the bucket of water. The shavings around the pot will burn, giving a reducing atmosphere and the water will prevent re-oxidation. A bucket of sand should be available for dousing any flames in an emergency.

Small raku kilns fired with solid fuel are quite easy to build as a further exercise in demonstrating the process of making low-fired pottery. The shell of the kiln could be constructed with fire-bricks. The muffle could be a saggar made with refractory clay using the slab technique and the principle of this type of kiln is illustrated in Fig. 77(b).

## Sawdust firing

This is the domestic version of the large open firings of primitive times. It is suitable for school field, or back-garden experiments, in producing very soft biscuit pots. When coming from the kiln these pots are often black with carbon deposits. If they are buffed, quite a high black shine can be produced, particularly if the pots have been burnished before firing. As the temperature during the firing reaches a maximum of only 500°–600°C, the resulting ware can hardly be called 'pot' and therefore is really only suitable for decoration. However, as an activity with children or students it is an inexpensive way of providing entertainment and pleasure. The procedure is as follows:

1   The kiln is built of bricks (fire-bricks preferably) which are arranged as shown in Fig. 77(a). The outside dimensions of this kiln are 2 ft × 2 ft × 3 ft (60 cm × 60 cm × 91 cm), but convenience is the only criterion here. A gap of approximately ½ in. (12.70 mm) should be left in between the bricks for air to get to the sawdust.
2   The bottom of the kiln should then be lined with a layer of dry sawdust to a depth of 4–6 in. (10.16–15.24 cm).

3   The first layer of greenware is then placed on the sawdust. The ware should be made from clay similar to raku ware and should be fairly robustly built. Any local clay with grog or sand in it would do for this low temperature firing. The largest shapes should make up the first layer, being placed approximately 2 in. (5.08 cm) apart with the same gap being left between the ware and the kiln wall. Hollow ware should be filled with sawdust and then the whole layer should be covered with more sawdust to a depth of 2–4 in. (5.08–10.16 cm).
4   Repeat this alternating process finishing up with a layer of sawdust just below the top of the kiln.
5   Place a paraffin-soaked rag over the top layer of sawdust and light it. Cover the kiln with an old metal dustbin lid, in case of rain. The lid should be punched with a few holes to help create a draught.

Initially the kiln will give off quite a lot of smoke, so make sure that you have either friendly neighbours or a reasonably sized piece of ground on which to site it. As the firing progresses the smoke will die down and the sawdust will continue to smoulder. The gaps between the bricks may have to be adjusted occasionally to make sure that this process continues. These adjustments can to some degree control the speed of the firing. The prevailing wind will also influence this.

As the layers of sawdust burn through, the pots will slowly fall down the kiln accumulating in a heap at the bottom. This is why the strongest pots were originally placed there. The firing can take anything between twelve and forty-eight hours depending on the size of kiln, etc. In any case the firing should be slow and a time of twenty-four hours would be about average.

When the firing is over the pots can be removed from the kiln and buffed. It may be noted that the slower the firing the blacker the pots will be.

## Summary

With the exception of the small experimental firings at the end of this chapter, I have assumed that normal firings will be carried out in kilns purchased from a manufacturer.

■ Sawdust forms.

Much has been written in pottery books about the building of one's own kiln (and other equipment). With plans, materials and know-how this is, as with many things, quite possible. However, before the building of one's own equipment can even be considered, a basic understanding of the purpose for which it is to be used must surely be the first priority.

Therefore, along with the information given in this book, practical experience is essential. For those not already engaged in the study of pottery-making, a part-time day or evening course at one of the many centres around the country is advisable. For a small enrolment fee one can at least become familiar with the basic requirements of materials and equipment.

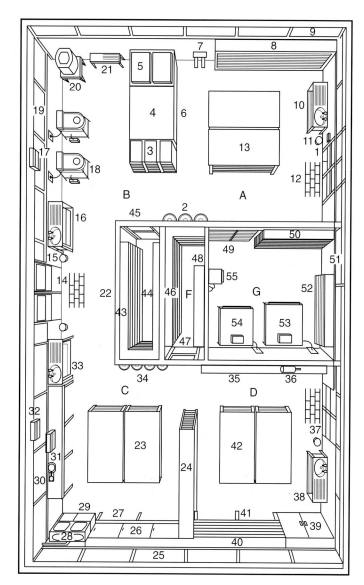

Fig. 78. A suggested layout for a pottery workshop.

### AREA A

**Clay working 1**

1 Swing door entrance
2 Clay reclamation bins
3 Clay storage boxes
4 Wedging bench
5 Plaster slabs
6 Underbench storage
7 Dod or wad box
8 Shelves for drying greenware
9 Windows to corridor or outside
10 Sink with clay trap
11 Roller paper towel and disposal bin
12 Ceramic-tiled floor throughout
13 Work benches with drawers for tools

### AREA B

**Clay working 2**

14 Swing door to outside
15 Roller paper towel and disposal bin
16 Sink with clay trap
17 Extractor fan
18 Power wheel
19 Outside windows
20 Blunger
21 Pug mill
22 Wall for display, etc.

### AREA C

**Glazing**

23 Work benches with drawers for tools
24 Shelves for biscuit ware
25 Windows to outside or corridor
26 Storage cupboards for oxides
27 Under bench storage
28 Spray booth with extractor to outside
29 Compressor unit
30 Window to outside
31 Scales on workbench
32 Extractor fan
33 Sink with clay trap
34 Bins for glazes

### AREA D

**Mould making**

35 Work bench
36 Lathe for plaster turning
37 Swing door entrance
38 Sink with clay trap
39 Drying cupboard for moulds, etc.
40 Shelves for storage of moulds
41 Under bench storage for plaster bins
42 Work benches with drawers for tools

### AREA E

**Damp storage**

43 Shelves for damp ware storage
44 Duck board floor to permit saturation
45 Sliding door

### AREA F

**Dry storage**

46 Shelves for storage of glazed ware
47 Sliding door
48 Entrance to kiln room

### AREA G

**Kilns**

49 Swing doors
50 Shelving for dry greenware awaiting biscuit
51 Windows to corridor or outside
52 Shelves for storage of kiln furniture
53 Large kiln
54 Small kiln
55 Test kiln

# Materials and equipment for the beginner

While many readers will sort out what materials and equipment they will require from the text, I have introduced the following list as a guide for those who might still be in doubt.

I have not given a costing as this would be out of date almost immediately. Send for the current catalogues and price lists from the suppliers (see page 114) and compare before ordering. Remember that, where possible, a comprehensive order to one firm will reduce package and carriage costs. Also, while all materials and equipment can be purchased from the listed suppliers, it might be possible to purchase some items locally (e.g. hessian, polythene sheeting, etc.) to save carriage costs.

If funds are not available for the quantities suggested in the list, then cuts will have to be made. Remember, however, that buying very small quantities is in the long run more costly than a large initial outlay.

I have assumed that suitable work surfaces are already available. Column 'A' suggests the requirements of one person setting up their own small workshop. Column 'B' suggests the requirements of a teacher beginning pottery with a class of twenty students.

| Description of items | A Quantity Imp. | A Quantity Metric | B Quantity Imp. | B Quantity Metric |
|---|---|---|---|---|
| *Kiln and accessories* | | | | |
| Kiln HT 1300°C | | | | |
|   (see page 00 and Fig. 00) | 1 | | 1 | |
| Kiln Furniture HT (usually supplied | | | | |
|   as an extra with kiln, comprising | | | | |
|   bats, props, stilts, spurs, etc.) | 1 set | | 1 set | |
| Standard pyrometer with thermocouple | 1 | | 1 | |
| Pyrometric cones (Staffordshire) | | | | |
|   Standard 01–1080°C | 50 | | 100 | |
|   1–1100°C | 50 | | 100 | |
|   2–1120°C | 50 | | 100 | |
|   8–1250°C | 50 | | 100 | |
| Sorting tool (for cleaning up pots and kiln | | | | |
|   furniture after firing) | 1 | | 1 | |
| Bat wash | 55 lb | 25 kg | 55 lb | 25 kg |
| Placing powder or sand | 55 | 25 | 55 | 25 |
| *Clay* | | | | |
| Red body plastic (maturing 1100°C–1160°C) | 220 lb | 100 kg | 330 lb | 150 kg |
| Buff earthenware/stoneware plastic | | | | |
|   (maturing earthenware, 1100°C–1160°C; | | | | |
|   maturing stoneware, 1220°C–1280°C) | 220 lb | 100 kg | 330 lb | 150 kg |
| Red body powdered (1100°C–1160°C) } for slips | 55 lb | 25 kg | 110 lb | 50 kg |
| White body powdered (1100°C–1160°C) } | 55 lb | 25 kg | 110 lb | 50 kg |
| Buff body powdered (1100°C–1280°C) } | 55 lb | 25 kg | 110 lb | 50 kg |
| White earthenware casting slip 1120°C– | | | | |
|   1160°C (only necessary if slip casting is | | | | |
|   intended) | 1 gal | 4.5 lit | 2 gal | 9.09 lit |
| Grog, 40–60 mesh | 55 lb | 25 kg | 55 lb | 25 kg |
| *Clay equipment* | | | | |
| Power or kick wheel (see Fig.0, page 00) | | | | |
|   (not essential at first) | 1 | | 4 | |
| 70-litre plastic bins (for reclaiming clay) | 3 | | 4 | |
| Workboards (plywood, chipboard): | | | | |
|   12 in. x 12 in. x ½ in. | | | | |
|   (305 mm x 305 mm x 13 mm); | 1 | | 20 | |
|   18 in. x 24 in. x ½ in. | | | | |
|   (460 mm x 610 mm x 13 mm); | 1 | | 10 | |
| Rolling-pins, hardwood | | | | |
|   14 in. (355 mm) working length | | | 10 | |
|   20 in. (510 mm) working length | 1 | | | |
| Rolling guides. lengths of wood | | | | |
|   ⅜ in. x 1 in. x 18 in. (9 mm x 25 mm | | | | |
|   x 460 mm) | 1 pr | | 10 prs | |

| Description of items | A Quantity Imp. | A Quantity Metric | B Quantity Imp. | B Quantity Metric |
|---|---|---|---|---|
| Clay cutters, 18 in. (4.57 mm) | 1 | | 10 | |
| Stainless steel or brass wire, (24 gauge | 1 coil | | 1 coil | |
|   for repairing clay cutters) | (½ lb) | (234 g) | (½ lb) | (234 g) |
| Boxwood modelling tools (usually | | | | |
|   supplied in sets of ten) | 1 set | | 2 sets | |
| Looped wire modelling tools | 2 | | 20 | |
| Rubber kidney palettes – medium | 1 | | 20 | |
| Steel kidney scrapers – medium | 1 | | 20 | |
| Turning tools (for wheelwork, usually | | | | |
|   supplied in sets of four) | 1 set | | 4 sets | |
| Callipers (usually for wheelwork) | 1 pr | | 4 prs | |
| Potter's knife | 1 | | 10 | |
| Lawns (for preparing slips): | | | | |
|   60 mesh, 10 in. (254 mm) | 1 | | 1 | |
|   80 mesh, 10 in. (254 mm) | 1 | | 1 | |
| Lawn brush (to be kept for preparing slips) | 1 | | 1 | |
| Hessian: | | | | |
|   3 ft x 2 ft (0.91 m x 0.60 m); | 1 length | | | |
|   3 ft x 40 ft (0.91 m x 12.1 m) | | | 1 length (into 20) | |
| Plastic sheeting, 250 gauge approx (for | see Cat. | | see Cat. | |
|   keeping greenware damp) | and local | | and local | |
| | stores | | stores | |
| Pugmill, electric, to mill about 4 cwts | | | | |
|   (255 kg) per hour (not essential at | | | | |
|   first but very useful) | 1 | | 1 | |
| *Glaze* | | | | |
| Transparent clear glaze (maturing | | | | |
|   1040°C–1150°C) | 55 lb | 25 kg | 110 lb | 50 kg |
| White opaque glaze (maturing 1040°C– | | | | |
|   1150°C) | 55 lb | 25 kg | 110 lb | 50 kg |
| Transparent glaze (maturing 1200°C– | | | | |
|   1280°C | 55 lb | 25 kg | 110 lb | 50 kg |
|   (Other raw materials for compiling | | | | |
|   one's own glazes and clays to recipes | | | | |
|   given in the text, can be purchased in | | | | |
|   similar quantities) | 55 lb | 25 kg | 55 lb | 25 kg |
| *Glaze equipment* | | | | |
| 2.2-gallon (10-litre) buckets with snap- | | | | |
|   on lids (for storage of glazes and slips) | 8 | | 10 | |
| 2-pt (1.1 litre) measuring jugs | 2 | | 4 | |
| Beam scales (to weigh from 1 g–5000) | 1 | | 1 | |

| Description of items | A Quantity Imp. | A Quantity Metric | B Quantity Imp. | B Quantity Metric |
|---|---|---|---|---|
| Cup lawn, 100 mesh | 1 | | 1 | |
| Lawn, 100 mesh 10 in. (254 mm) diameter (to be used only for glazes) | 1 | | 1 | |
| Lawn brush (to be used only for glazes) | 1 | | 1 | |
| *Colouring and decoration materials* | | | | |
| Cobalt oxide | 2.2 lb | 1 kg | 4.4 lb | 2 kg |
| Copper oxide | 2.2 lb | 1 kg | 4.4 lb | 2 kg |
| Manganese dioxide | 2.2 lb | 1 kg | 4.4 lb | 2 kg |
| Iron oxide (red) | 4.4 lb | 2 kg | 8.8 lb | 4 kg |
| Selection of five underglaze colours | 3.5 oz (of each) | 100 g (of each) | 7.0 oz (of each) | 200 g (of each) |
| Underglaze medium (not essential as water will do, but helps to prevent smudging) | 1 pt | 0.57 lit | 2 pt | 1.14 lit |
| Other colouring agents can be ordered in similar or larger quantities if and when required. On-glaze enamel colours with the necessary oil medium can be ordered in similar quantities to underglaze colours if required. | | | | |
| *Decorating Equipment* | | | | |
| Majolica pencils, size 2, length of hair 16 mm | 1 | | 20 | |
| size 6, length of hair 22 mm | 1 | | 20 | |
| One stroke, ½ in. (13 mm), length of hair 26 mm | 1 | | 20 | |
| Flat lacquer brush, 1 in. (25.4 mm) length of hair 27 mm | 1 | | 5 | |
| Mop, size 6, length of hair 38 mm | 1 | | 5 | |
| Slip trailers, bulb-shaped with detachable nozzles (large) | 3 | | 20 | |
| *Miscellaneous items* | | | | |
| Bench whirlers, cast iron, 10 in. x 6 in. (254 mm x 152 mm) | 1 | | 5 | |
| Natural sponges, medium | 1 | | 5 | |
| Synthetic sponges (small) | 1 | | 20 | |
| Synthetic sponges (large) for bench cleaning | 1 | | 10 | |
| Bench scrapers | 1 | | 5 | |
| Palette knives, 6 in. x 1 in. (152 mm x 25 mm) blade (for mixing colours, etc.) | 1 | | 5 | |

| Description of items | A Quantity Imp. | A Quantity Metric | B Quantity Imp. | B Quantity Metric |
|---|---|---|---|---|
| Ceramic tiles, gloss white, 6 in. x 6 in. (152 mm x 152 mm) (for mixing colours on) | 2 | | 20 | |
| Round bowls, plastic, 14 in. x 5 in. (355 mm x 127 mm) for general use | 3 | | 6 | |
| Plastic containers (with screw or tight-fitting lids for storing oxides, colours, etc. capacity approx. 2.2 lb (1 kg)) | 10 | | 20 | |
| Scoops, plastic, 9 in. x 5 ¾ in. (229 mm x 146 mm) | | | 3 | |
| Surform plane (small) with spare blades (for trimming leather hard clay and plastic edges) (not availiable from general suppliers) | 3 | | 5 | |
| Scissors (small) for stencil work, etc. (not available from general supplier) | 1 pr | | 20 prs | |
| Rulers (imp. and metric) not available from general supplier | 1 | | 20 | |
| Gummed labels, for labelling materials (not available from general suppliers) | 1 box | | 1 box | |
| Transparent adhesive, for making labels waterproof | 1 roll | | 1 roll | |
| Plaster of Paris (for plaster slabs and moulds) | 110 lb | 50 kg | 220 lb | 100 kg |
| Mould-makers size (for mould-making) | 2.2 lb | 1 kg | 2.2 lb | 1 kg |
| Sodium silicate | 1.1 lb | 0.5 kg | 2.2 lb | 1 kg |
| Soda Ash | 1.1 lb | 0.5 kg | 2.2 lb | 1 kg |
| { Only required if it is intended to make one's own casting slip from the text recipe | | | | |
| Cottle sheeting (or linoleum) and suitable lengths of timber (see text, page 30, Making a Plaster Slab) will be required if it is intended to make moulds. Ready-made bat moulds and cottle sheeting can be purchased from general supplier. | | | | |
| A supply of strong elastic bands for split moulds and cottles (cut-up car and cycle inner tubes are good) | | | | |
| Wax emulsion resist (for preventing glaze adhering to the bottom of biscuit pots and for resist decoration) | 1 pt | 0.57 lit | 2 pt | 1.14 lit |
| Lengths of wood similar to rolling guides (for stirring glazes, slips, etc.) | 10 | | 10 | |
| Garden cane, 6 ft x ⅜ in. (1.82 m x 10 mm) approx, for making incising and sgraffito tools. | 1 lgth | | 2 lgths | |

# Suppliers of pottery materials and equipment

## U.K. Suppliers

- Pottery Crafts Ltd., Campbell Road, Stoke-on-Trent, Staffordshire. ST4 7ET.
- Potclays Ltd., Brickkiln Lane, Etruria, Stoke-on-Trent, Staffordshire. ST4 7BP.
- Kilns and Furnaces Ltd., Unit 1, Cinderhill Trading Estate, Coney Road, Stoke-on-Trent, Staffordshire. ST3 5JU.
- The Cromartie Group, Park Hull Road, Longton, Stoke-on Trent, Staffordshire. ST3 5AT.
- Ceram Research (for glaze safety testing), Queen's Road, Penkull, Stoke-on-Trent, Staffordshire.

For additional information contact Ceramic Review, the magazine of the Craft Potters Association of Great Britain, 21 Carnaby Street, London. W1V 1PH.

## Overseas Suppliers

These can be contacted through the following organisations/publications.

### Australia

- *Pottery in Australia*, 2/68 Alexander Street, Crows Nest, New South Wales, 2065.
- *Ceramics, Art and Perception*, 35 William Street, Paddington, New South Wales 2021.

### Canada

- Canadian Crafts Federation, c/o Ontario Crafts Council, Designers Walk, 170 Bedford Road, Suite 300, Toronto M5R 2K9.
- Canadian Ceramics Society, 2175 Sheppard Avenue East, Suite 310, Willowdale, Ontario, M21 1W8.

### New Zealand

- *New Zealand Potter*, P.O. Box 881, Auckland, New Zealand.

### South Africa

- *National Ceramics Quarterly*, P.O. Box 568, Anerly, Natal 4230.

### U.S.A.

- *Ceramics Monthly*, 735 Ceramic Place, Westerville, Ohio, 43081.

# Taking it further

Art Deco and Modernist Ceramics
K. McCready
Thames and Hudson          ISBN 0 500 27825 3

Ash Glazes
P. Rogers
A & C Black          ISBN 0 713 63440 5

Clay and Glazes for the Potter
D. Rhodes
A & C Black          ISBN 0 801 95633 1

Coiled Pottery
B. Blandino
A & C Black          ISBN 0 713 64523 7

Contemporary Porcelain
P. Lane
A & C Black          ISBN 0 713 63956 3

The Craft and Art of Clay
S. Peterson
King          ISBN 1 856 69069 5

The Encyclopedia of Pottery Techniques
P. Cosentino
Headline Books          ISBN 0 747 27889 X

A Guide to Public Collections of Studio Pottery in the British Isles
R. Fournier
Ceramic Review          ISBN 0 950 47679 X

Handmade Tiles
S. Giorgini
David & Charles          ISBN 0 715 30338 4

Illustrated Dictionary of Practical Pottery
R. Fournier
A & C Black          ISBN 0 173 63152 5

The Mosaic Book
P. Vance/C. Goodrick-Clarke
Conran Octopus          ISBN 1 850 29658 8

The Potters Art
G. Clarke
Phaidon          ISBN 0 714 83202 2

A Potters Book
B. Leach
Faber & Faber          ISBN 0 571 10973 X

Raku, A Practical Approach
S. Branfman
A & C Black          ISBN 0 713 63473 1

Raku, The Way of
C. Herrman
Pattern Press          ISBN 0 950 76897 0

Salt Glaze Ceramics
J. Mansfield
Craftsman House          ISBN 0 713 63582 7

*Slipware*
M. Wondraush
A & C Black                    ISBN 0 713 62813 8

*Smashing Pots: Feats of Clay from Africa*
N. Barley
British Museum Press           ISBN 0 714 12513 X

*Smoke Fired Pottery*
J. Perryman
A & C Black                    ISBN 0 713 63882 6

*Studio Pottery*
O. Watson
Phaidon                        ISBN 0 714 82948 X

*Tin Glazed Earthenware*
D. Carnegy
A & C Black                    ISBN 0 801 98487 4

I have compiled the above book list for your further enjoyment and knowledge of pottery. The ISBN number will help you to order the books through your local bookshop if they are not in stock, or by visiting or contacting the following addresses.

- Crafts Council Gallery Shop, 44a Pentonville Road, London N1 9BY. Tel. 0171 806 2558

- Contemporary Ceramics, Craft Potters Shop and Gallery, 7 Marshall Street, London W1V 1LP. Tel. 0171 437 7605

- Victoria and Albert Museum, Craft Shop, South Kensington, London SW7 2RL. Tel. 0171 938 8438

Further information about pottery/ceramics, classes, seminars and available reading etc. can be obtained from museums, galleries, art and craft shops, libraries, ceramics magazines and suppliers' catalogues.

# Acknowledgements

I would like to thank Mrs Joan Foers for so capably typing the manuscript and Mr Keith Heppell for his efficient photographic work which appears throughout the book. Illustrations are from originals by John Gale.

I would also like to thank the many people who have helped me to get so much enjoyment out of making pottery, both as a student at the Central School of Art, and since then. I hope that this book will help others to do the same.

## About the Author

Originally trained in Art and Design and Ceramics at the Central School of Art in London, John Gale has considerable experience as an artist and teacher. As a lecturer in Ceramics at an Art School and the Head of Art at a Comprehensive School he is an ideal author of Pottery. His credits are numerous, ranging from *Pebble Mill at One* on BBC1, Channel 4 and Tyne Tees Television to an exhibition at Sotheby's, London. He has work in many private collections worldwide.

 John Gale

# Index